New Attitude, New Job:

Tools to Inspire

Self-Esteem, Resilience, Success

by Graehme Hall

Hermaden Press

©2016

New Attitude, New Job:

Tools to Inspire

Self-Esteem, Resilience, Success

because you are meant

to be successful!

This book was written for a variety of readers, each one with a unique set of circumstances. Not every example will be applicable to all readers. Take what works for you!

With much appreciation to Ferdinand Stöhr for his magnificent photo that served as the basis and inspiration for the cover art. And many thanks to Sister Betty Coveney for encouraging the print edition of this book.

ISBN: 978-0-9854284-2-6

ISBN-10: 0-9854284-2-2

Library of Congress Control Number: 2016920283

Hermaden Press
Glen Ellyn, Illinois

www.hermaden.com

First e-book edition March 2012

First print edition December 2016

To Mark and Rebecca,

With deep appreciation

for all your support and love

Table of Contents

Preface

My business focuses on personal empowerment. Part of my work has been teaching personal empowerment classes at a local community center. I noticed that people who were taking my courses and were unemployed -- or wanting a better job -- were usually finding those jobs within weeks, even if they had been unemployed many months. They were often giving credit to the class for helping them pivot to a better-feeling place that allowed them to connect with their desired job. They felt better about themselves. They started focusing on strengths and successes instead of weaknesses and failures. Sometimes they gained clarity about the type of work or career they were seeking. They were reconnecting with the essence of who they really are. They started seeing themselves differently. Their innate resilience rose.

If you put a piece of cork in water, it will float. But if you press it down under the water, it will stay there until you remove your finger. Then the cork rises again.

People are like that cork. If we start feeling down, depressed, defeated, we develop patterns of thought that keep us under water: essentially drowning. If, however, we change our habits of thinking and start thinking better thoughts, we naturally rise to the top again.

We do our own thinking. This means we can intentionally choose to change the way we think. No one can do this for us. We must undertake the change ourselves.

We all know the cliché that we take ourselves with us wherever we go. We cannot escape what we think, but we can change what we think. Because what we think matters. A lot.

If you have been looking for employment, seeking a better job, or trying to find a new career path and have not achieved the results you want, consider changing your most important tool: your mind. Your perspective of yourself and the world is more crucial than you may ever have realized.

This book was originally written for people who were long-term job seekers, perhaps who had been unemployed for a while or were returning to the job market after a period of alternate focus. It was published as an e-book to make it affordable. Then I started hearing from people who were sharing the book with high school and college students who were looking for their first full-time job. Individuals who were already employed said this book helped to boost their attitude and self-confidence so they found a better job. So now the e-book has been converted into a workbook with space to write many of the exercises. The style is conversational – not always correct grammatically, but more personal, like we might have if the two of us were talking.

Parts of this book may apply to you; parts may not. Find what feels right and resonates with you. Some exercises, or tools, may appeal one day and not another. Look for the tools that will work for you.

It doesn't take a big book to help you make big changes. It does take mental work, though, to change habits of thought. The exercises in this book are designed to help you achieve a new consciousness of success: *your success.* But practice them you must. Tools are only helpful when actually used. Reading a book is different than applying its principles. Your success begins in your mind. To take any journey, you must begin it. Advance to the next page, and begin a new journey in your life.

Introduction

Getting a new job is not just about qualifications, credentials, and experience. It is also the mindset you carry through the process. It is the mindset with which you approach applying and interviewing. You present to a hiring manager, just as you do a résumé, how you feel about yourself, your past employers, and the possibility of working for this organization. You are sharing your perspective and outlook on life, the stories you tell yourself and others, the kind of attitude you will bring to the work environment every day. These aspects may not be visible on paper, but they are being "read" just the same.

Are you a fit for the company? Are you a match to what already exists, or what the organization is seeking to create? Do your current attributes indicate future success? Employers may read your résumé and evaluate your responses to questions, but they are also using other tools to assess your suitability for the position and the organization.

We have all known people who were hired because the interviewer "had a good feeling" about the person. We have known job seekers who felt, as soon as they entered the room, as if the interviewer didn't like them: "I knew I wasn't going to be called back."

No one is a fit, a match, to every job applied for. Nor, frankly, would one want to be. Many of us have had jobs that, in hindsight, we wish we hadn't experienced.

But the longer we are on the job market, the more our zeal to keep looking can erode. The more news we hear about a difficult economy, the sooner many recent graduates are ready to give up. How can you recover? How can you find, not only resilience, but a great job?

People will often say to me, "I've been looking for a job for X months." And I will, annoyingly, ask them: "Have you spent this time *looking* for a job, or *finding* a job?" There is actually a huge difference in the approach.

When we get in the mindset of looking, we often stop *finding*. We look for jobs to apply for. We put in applications. We complete the tests, submit the forms, and do whatever is necessary to qualify for consideration. After a while, with only silence or rejection for our hard work, we don't expect any more that we will hear back. We may still be doing the legwork of applying, but we have stopped expecting positive results.

After even more time, we stop putting in as many applications. We use a generic cover letter instead of personalizing it, or we don't include a cover letter at all. We don't finish all the tests or we take them less seriously. We begin to take an attitude like, "You're not going to hire me anyway, so what's the point?" We stop expecting success.

We listen to the news. We decide there are many reasons we're not being hired, and we're hearing it from "experts" after all. Many reasons are more personal than just the condition of the economy. We're too young or too old. We're overqualified or underqualified. Too much experience or too little. Not the right credentials for the job, too few or too many. We're too soon out of school, or too long out of school. Too much education or too little. There always seems to be something wrong with *us*. Yes, the experts give us many reasons why we can't find a job. And we believe them.

The title of this book is not meant to imply you don't have a job because your attitude is faulty. You may have a great attitude. However, spending a long time on the job market can wear down that great attitude. This book is about *renewing* your attitude: refreshing and reinvigorating it. It's about learning to tell a new story, a better story, about yourself, your present and your future.

When I was a kid, I had a *Bozo the Clown* bop bag. This was an inflatable toy punching bag about four feet tall with a weighted bottom. It had a picture of Bozo on its front. You blew it up, stood it on the floor in front of you, and then you punched it. It was a child's stress reliever. Of course, you didn't just punch it once. You hit it again and again and again.

Being on the job market for a long time can feel like being that bop bag. You start out feeling tall, with high hopes. You feel shiny and strong and new. Then you start getting rejected. And rejected. Again and again. Each time is like you are being hit a little harder.

After a while, the bop bag starts to lose air. It is slower to bounce back.

Keep hitting the bop bag, and eventually it won't come back at all. It has lost its resilience. It is too deflated to bounce back.

As human beings, we say to ourselves that we have to keep bouncing back. We have to keep looking. We have to look until we find something. It just gets harder and harder to keep looking, harder and harder to be enthusiastic, harder and harder to be hopeful.

That's where a new attitude comes in. We have to pick *ourselves* up off the floor, so to speak. We need some air.

3

Unlike the bop bag, we have a conscious perspective that we determine. We can change our focus. We can change our attitude. We can change our approach and *how we feel.*

We have to start feeling better, or nothing else in our lives is going to change.

Do you want to feel better?

Okay, that may sound like a stupid question. Try this one: Do you *believe* you can feel better?

Can you, at least, *have hope* that you can feel better?

Whether you have a job or not, you can choose to feel better. Right now. In this moment. You can decide: I want to feel better.

You're been working at finding a job. Are you willing to work to feel better?

You would be surprised how often, when you start feeling better, new ideas come. New possibilities emerge. New doors open.

I can't guarantee that a new attitude is going to mean a new job. I can tell you that, with or without a job, you might as well start to feel better.

I can tell you that many people, when they start feeling better, do find a new job or create other ways to produce income.

Often, when we feel like that deflated bop bag, we wait for someone else to come in and inflate us. Sometimes, we want to be rescued. Well, the surest way to recover is to *rescue yourself.* Unlike the bop bag, you can choose to get back up. You can choose to think differently about yourself, your situation, your future. ONLY YOU can get inside your mind. ONLY YOU can decide: I am willing to try thinking differently. After all, what do you have to lose? Feeling miserable? Feeling unworthy? Those are feelings we can all live without.

A new attitude takes work to develop. It takes effort. Many people undertake a new attitude like a new diet. They start out strong, and by the second or third day, they're slipping. By the end of the first or second week, the intention for a new attitude is a long-lost memory. Fitness centers capitalize on people who undertake a new year's resolution in January to work out. Better sign that individual up for the whole year now, because that person probably won't be seen in the gym after January.

Why isn't intention enough?

Have you ever seen a muddy dirt road after heavy rain? If you've ever driven a car down a road like that, you know that one set of tire tracks emerges in the road. The first driver creates a path through the mud. The next driver gets his tires in the same tracks. The third driver does the same with her tires. You can see where the drivers went before you. You believe the path of least resistance is to do the same: just follow in their tracks. You get a good set of ruts in the road, and it's a lot easier to follow than to create a new path.

Have you ever tried to step around a big puddle, or through muddy grass, after a rainstorm? If someone else has gone before us trying to avoid the puddle and we see footprints, we naturally put our feet in those prints. We don't give it much thought. We may not consider whether this is the best course for us to follow. We see that others have stepped around the puddle before us, and we follow their path.

Our minds are like that. We develop patterns of thinking, and we get ruts set into the road and into our brains. We have to free ourselves to think differently. Is it a little harder to maneuver the car at first if we don't drive in those old ruts? Of course. But we might also discover new, firmer ground where we didn't think there was any before. We might discover those old ruts weren't the best path for us to take.

Do you remember in school reading Robert Frost's poem about two roads that diverged in the woods? The speaker says he took the one "less traveled by" and that's what made the difference in his life. You are about to embark on a road less traveled. You are going to create a new mental path, a new mental pattern, for yourself. As you do this, you will start to feel better. As you start to feel better, you will begin to notice little changes in your life, little improvements. That will help affirm that you are on the right path. Gradually, you will notice bigger improvements. Like a new job. New income.

This is not a "ten days to a better you" program. You have to keep working at it. You have to let it become habit. Let yourself become so positive that you annoy the people around you. Let yourself become so good at finding the silver lining that you don't complain about the clouds anymore. Heck, you don't even *see* the clouds anymore. "Wow, look at that beautiful silver lining up in the sky." Yes, you may really annoy some people. And won't that be great?! It can be a lot of fun to be annoyingly positive. (Trust me: I know.)

So, you might be asking, "How do I do it?"

Well, first you must realize that what you think matters. We tend to attract more in our lives of what we give our attention to. If I give my attention to a shortage of jobs and I believe there is a shortage of jobs, then I am talking myself out of looking and applying. You just need one job. *One job!* The national economy doesn't matter. Your state's economy doesn't matter. You just have to connect with one good-paying job. This is not about improving the national economy; this is about improving your personal economy. You are not dependent on Congress to pass a bill for you. You don't need millions of new jobs created. You just have to find that single job.

Forget about the other people applying. Leave them out of it. If you start comparing yourself to others, you will probably find ways you think you come up short. You will diminish yourself. When you think less of yourself, when you expect an interviewer not to waste his or her time with you: well, if you don't think highly of yourself, why should anyone else, either?

Many successful people have talked about how they *felt* successful *before* they actually *achieved* their success. They felt special. They felt driven. They were determined. They knew, somewhere inside, that they were meant to live life on a grand scale. They felt a mission, a calling. However this feeling translated to these individuals, the commonality was that they *felt successful before they were.* They would walk down the street and think, "Don't these people know who I am?" And only then would they remember: *not yet!*

This is *success consciousness.* They have the consciousness of a successful person, even if it has not manifested in their lives yet. The stories they think and tell themselves are the stories of success. Like energies attract. You need to adopt the consciousness of someone successfully employed. *You are going to find a job. You are going to connect with a new source of income.* Feel it. Believe it. Know it to be true. Your future employer may not know it yet, but they are going to hire you. And they are going to be lucky to have you, too!

The Toolbox

This book contains exercises for you to do. You can start right out and do them one at a time, or flip through the book and find one that resonates with you. This will be your toolbox until you find and start your new job. Try to make time each day to practice some of these exercises. This is part of your job-finding work.

You need to spend more time thinking optimistically than pessimistically. You need to spend more time realizing your job is already out there than feeling a job is elusive. You need to spend more time each day thinking positively about yourself than negatively about yourself.

This extends to the people and activities in your life, too. Do you hang around people who build you up, or tear you down? Do the people in your life support you emotionally, or feel like a drain on you?

Do you engage in activities that feel good to you? Do you listen to music with upbeat lyrics? Do you watch television shows that empower you? Do you see movies that inspire you? Do you read books that uplift you? Start paying attention to what you're giving your attention. Become mindful. Get conscious about the thoughts you're thinking.

Stop watching the news, especially economic news. You don't have to stay "informed." It is much more important that you feel hopeful and expect your life to move in a positive direction.

Tell your friends and family members to stop asking how the job search is going. Even though they may be well-intentioned, it is demoralizing for you to keep answering that you have not found a job yet. Tell them that you will let them know when you find something. If you want to, tell them you are developing a new plan and strengthening your interview skills. You are taking a new approach. Then say, "After I have the job, I'll tell you how I did it."

If you have borrowed money from family and friends to get through this difficult time, they may feel they have a right to details. But what matters most right now is that you get into a better place mentally and emotionally. Be kind and thoughtful. Tell them how much you value their help. Explain to them that you are bouncing back, finding a new strength to double your efforts, and you appreciate their generous support. Let them know you are more hopeful than ever that you will start repaying them soon.

What sometimes happens is that a person will start feeling more positive and enthusiastically share the feeling with other people before the new mental ruts, so to speak, are fully developed. Other people will criticize or tear down the new approach, the new you. When you build a brick wall, you wait for the cement to settle before you put weight on it. Wait until you feel strong in your new attitude and fortified in your approach before you reach out to others. If it still doesn't succeed, just stop sharing: don't stop doing the work.

Spend at least 51% (or more) of your time each day focused on thoughts that help you feel good about yourself. Take a positive approach to job searches and applications. Think ahead to the interview and prepare. Your mindset will help you get that job, and help you be successful once you have it.

To do the exercises in this book, you may want to get a notebook or journal, create a new file on your computer or tablet, or simply get a folder and put individual sheets of paper in it. Just don't wait to start: begin now.

My Success List

Make a list of *at least* ten times in your life when you felt successful. It doesn't matter how big or small the successes were. It doesn't matter how far back you reach. Start with ten. Then expand the list over time. Add to it.

Once you have found ten, you will begin to think of others you can add. This is an ongoing project. Remind yourself of these successes at least once each day. Read through your list. Remember how it felt. Re-experience those successes as if they were happening *right now*.

No matter how young or old we are, we have past successes. Parents consider it a huge accomplishment when children take their first steps. If you were physically able, you probably learned to walk, right? That's a success. You graduated from at least one school. Maybe you learned to ride a bike or drive a car. Remember how good it felt to have that freedom? Remember how great it was to head out on your own? You felt on top of the world.

If you have held a job before, then you have been hired before. Or maybe you were an entrepreneur and had your own lemonade stand or newspaper route. Did you ever sell any products for your school? Each of those was a success. Did you ever play sports? Have hobbies? Any successes there? It doesn't matter if others recognized you as being successful. It only matters that *you felt successful*.

You need to remind yourself of past successes. You need to remember that future successes are ahead of you. You know how to succeed. You've done it many times before!

My Success List

Times in my life I felt successful:

1)

2)

3)

4)

5)

6)

7)

8)

9)

10)

11)

12)

13)

14)

15)

My Abundance List

Usually when people have been searching for a job for a while, money is also on their minds. Make a list of at least ten times in your life when you experienced financial abundance: you felt *rich!* Maybe it was when you received your first paycheck. Maybe you bought something you had wanted for a long time. Maybe you came into some unexpected money: perhaps you received it as a gift, or even found it. Maybe you bought your first vehicle or your first home. Maybe it was the first time you rented an apartment. You felt you had *accomplished something.* You had money to get what you wanted.

Do you remember when you were a little kid, before you knew how much things cost? A dollar seemed like a lot of money. If you were given $1, $5, or $10, you felt rich! You thought you could buy anything with that money. It was a lot of money to you back then. Remember the feeling of it.

If you want to feel rich again, give a small child a dollar. (Make sure it is okay with his or her parent first, of course.) Look at the child's eyes light up. Look at how much enthusiasm the child has for one dollar. Remember when you felt that way?

Just as with the *Success List,* get inside these stories. Relive the feelings as if you are experiencing them for the first time. Add to these lists as new memories and feelings come to you. Start spending time every day reminding yourself that you have known success and abundance, and you will again.

My Abundance List

Times in my life I had a feeling of abundance: I felt rich, or like I could buy/do something I wanted.

1)

2)

3)

4)

5)

6)

7)

8)

9)

10)

11)

12)

13)

14)

15)

My Resilience List

Anyone who is old enough to be looking for a job has had times in his or her life when things did not go as planned or wanted. Maybe we lost something or someone that was important to us. Maybe we did not do as well at a task or accomplishment as we had hoped. Maybe we set out to achieve something, but failed or stopped before reaching our goal. We all have had those experiences.

What we did next, however, is where we need to focus now. When you fall off a bicycle, you get back on and try riding again. Maybe not at first, but eventually. If you're in a car accident, you drive again. If you are hurt in a relationship, you eventually start dating again. We all have times when we struggle, then somehow manage to pick ourselves back up and keep going.

This list is for times you were resilient. Don't focus on the problem that caused the situation, but *focus on the solution*. Focus on the fact that *you kept going*!

How many people are happily in a relationship now, but can remember times it seemed as if love was lost forever? How many people started a class or course in school that was hard or even incomprehensible, and not only got through it but developed a new understanding or passion? We all have the capacity for resilience. In this exercise, recall times where, even though you felt overwhelmed, lost, despair, defeated: you kept going. You kept going, and somehow, things worked out.

When a person we love dies, we often lose ourselves in grief. Depression may follow. But we eventually can emerge on the other side and find a new normal if we keep going.

Losing a job, or having a hard time finding a new job, can feel similar. We can feel loss. We can grieve, especially if we are no longer at a job important to our self-identity. Think about the times in your life when you felt hopeless but pulled through. You kept going, and you made it to better, happier times again.

Your situation right now is temporary and you need to remember that. We can start to feel like it is permanent. We can start to feel that better times are not ahead. Well, they are. You need to keep going. You have encountered difficulties before, but you didn't let them define you. These challenges are not you. You are better than that. You are stronger than that. You did not give up before. Why would you give up now? Think about those times you did not give up and realize that same strength is within you. In fact, you are older and wiser, more experienced now than you were then. You have more to draw from *now*.

Don't give credit in your earlier recoveries to other people. Don't write it off as luck. It was you. You kept going. You made it through. You made it to the other side, and you will this time.

Start with a list of six times you have recovered: six times when you were resilient. After you remember those six, see if you can find a seventh. An eighth. Add to the list as long as it feels good to you. Stay focused on the solution. Stay focused on the fact that you did it. You recovered and rose. And you will again.

My Resilience List

Times in my life I was resilient, when I kept going:

1)

2)

3)

4)

5)

6)

7)

8)

9)

10)

11)

12)

13)

14)

15)

Get Back to Dreaming and Envisioning

We can become so fixated on our present, especially our current dilemmas, that we forget about our future. We can feel so desperate in the present moment that we forget: it won't always feel this way. We need to get back to dreaming. We need to get back to envisioning the future we want for ourselves and our families.

This is not an exercise in *what I think I can have,* or *what I think I can achieve.* This is a dream exercise. If you could live your fantasy life, what would it be? Where would you live? How would you spend your days, your nights, your weekends? How would you *feel* in that life? You can close your eyes right now and start imagining.

If you say, "I don't know what I want," then think about how you would want to *feel* in your fantasy. Most of us want to feel loved and appreciated. We want to spend our days doing things that feel meaningful to us, that we enjoy and find value in. We want to spend time doing what we enjoy. We want to be happy. We may want people and animals in our lives to love, who also love us. How would you want to feel in your fantasy life? Don't stop your imaginative process with don'ts or can'ts. This is play. This is pretend. This is creating your ideal.

Now, let's find ways to make the fantasy *feel* real. Make a creation/inspiration board or box. You might take a piece of poster board or cardboard, or a bulletin board. You could choose a box, basket, or jar. Choose something that feels right.

Then start selecting images that represent the feelings you want in your future. If you know specifics, select images that represent exactly what you desire. If there is a certain car or truck you want, for instance, find a picture of it or print one out from the internet. If you are single and you want a family, find pictures of happy families. The images and words can be what you want, or represent the feeling that you want.

Find pictures, words, descriptions, whatever is meaningful to you. Post them on the board or put them in your container. Only spend time on this activity when you are willing to let yourself play. Have fun with this! Wouldn't it be wonderful to spend time here? To travel to this place? This is your fantasy future. Enjoy it.

You need to let yourself play with the creation of your future. You need to let your imagination roam and run. Add to your creation over time. See something you want in your dream house? Add it. Go to web sites that represent the future you want. Print out pictures that capture the essence of your vision.

As mentioned earlier in this book, don't share this with people who won't appreciate it. This is for you. In your mind, live the fantasy. Make it real. It is okay to let yourself want something, even if you don't see a way right now that you will ever achieve it. It is okay to dream, even if that dream is far away from your current reality. We have to give ourselves permission to think big, and think outside the box of our present. If you could have anything, what would it be? If you could live your life any way you desire, how would you live? Imagine. Explore. *Have fun!*

Dreaming and Envisioning

The feelings I experience living in my fantasy life, in my dream life, are:

Release Blame, Choose Empowerment

A pattern of blame can keep you from getting a job. Why? Because when you are actively blaming someone or something, you keep yourself tied to it. Whatever happened, it is in the past. If you were fired from your last job, or your company downsized, you may still be angry. You may be blaming your boss, the company, the president, the economy. You may be blaming yourself.

Anger can occasionally help us feel a little better in the short term. It feels better to be angry with someone else than to feel like we did something wrong, for instance.

But blame ties us to the past. It ties us to what was. It doesn't let us focus on the future.

Blame can imply powerlessness. When you blame others for you not having a job, you are giving your power of a job to them. You are saying, in essence: *This person took my job away from me. This person has my job.* No, they don't. There are lots of jobs out there. There are lots of opportunities for your future you may not let yourself see if you stay tied to the past. You have to focus forward, not backward. You have to look ahead to the future, not back to the past. The past is over. It is done. There is nothing you can do to change it. What you can change is your attitude about the future. What you can change is the direction you're facing, and the way you are facing it.

You have at least two possibilities, if you are still actively blaming someone. The first is that, when you have a thought of blame arise, you redirect the thought. Stop that thought in the moment and replace it with a better thought. Be aware that simply stopping a thought is not enough. You need to change your focus. You need to have another thought that becomes your new habit.

The second possibility is to resolve how you are feeling about the situation or person. Either way, you need to stop old patterns of blame and replace those thoughts with better-feeling, non-blaming thoughts.

Examples

Old thought: I shouldn't have been fired.

New thought: Why would I want to keep working for a company that doesn't appreciate me? Now I can find a better job where I am really valued.

Old thought: It wasn't fair that they didn't honor my seniority and replaced me with someone who was younger and less costly to the company.

New thought: I have lots of experience and wisdom to offer a new company. My former employer is going to miss me, even if they haven't figured that out yet and never tell me. I am really good at what I do. I am looking forward to working for a company that realizes I can accomplish more in less time because of my experience. I'm a real asset.

Old thought: Those personnel directors never want to hire someone who is just out of school and doesn't have experience yet. How am I supposed to get experience if I can't get a job?

New thought: I am so eager and have so much to offer a new company. I know there are hiring managers who will recognize my enthusiasm. I am going to work hard and make them glad they took a chance. It isn't even taking a chance, because I am determined to do a great job.

Old thought: I was so stupid to drop out of school and not finish my degree. Nobody wants to hire someone who doesn't have a degree.

New thought: I was choosing what I thought was best for me at the time. I can go back to school if I really want to. I have heard of people finishing their degree in their nineties. It really is never too late. If I don't want to go back to school, that's okay, too. I can take an entry-level job and work myself up. Maybe I could look for a company that will help pay for my education if they like my work. Degrees don't really measure a person's competence or creativity. Many tremendously successful people have dropped out of school. It really doesn't say much at all about who I am or what I have to offer a company.

Old thought: If my supervisor had just covered for me the way I asked him to, and not reported all the times I was late, I would still have a job. Why couldn't he cover for me? It's his fault I lost that job.

New thought: Well, I was the one being late, even if I felt like I couldn't help it at the time. I know it was my supervisor's responsibility to report attendance and who was late. He was just doing his job. I can appreciate he didn't want to get fired because I was late. I was the one who was late, after all, not him. He was really good about showing up on time. Yes, I guess it wasn't his fault. And I understand now, in a new way, why it is important to be on time. This has been a lesson I won't forget. I know I'm human and sometimes things happen in life that we don't predict. But when I start my next job, I think I will plan to be early every day. Then if I run into difficulty getting there, at least I'll be on time. I may have more life responsibilities than many people do, but I know other people handle their responsibilities and still get to work on time. I guess I can, too.

When you have an interview for a new job and you are asked why your previous position ended or why you have been unemployed so long, it is important you are not blaming someone: even yourself. Interviewers can be very good at detecting *meta messages*: the non-verbal communication that accompanies the words we are actually saying. You may not verbalize blame, but you can still communicate it.

Interviewers realize that someone who is looking backward is not looking forward. Energy spent in blame is not energy spent moving their company successfully into the future. You need to start spending your time in ways that are valuable to you and help you move forward. Blame ties you to the past. That is not what is ahead of you, unless you choose to keep re-creating it. Let the past go, and focus your energies on what you can and will become in the future.

Replacing Old Thoughts of Blame
with New Thoughts of Empowerment

Old thought:

New thought:

Old thought:

New thought:

Old thought:

New thought:

Old thought:

New thought:

Lifting Limitations

Other than blame, are you are placing limitations on yourself that may be keeping you from getting a new job? Are you keeping yourself trapped...and unemployed? What thoughts are limiting you?

For instance, if you can't find a job locally and believe you can't move to a new location, you may be boxing yourself in. If you need to live near an aging relative you care for, you may not have considered that you could move both of you if necessary. If you think there is only one employer in your town that can give you a job, and that company turned you down or fired you, you may be giving up.

It's important to lift limitations in your thinking and allow new possibilities to emerge. Play the "what if" game. Think about any beliefs you might have that you feel are standing in your way. And then wonder, "What if...?"

For instance, maybe you live in the city and don't have a reliable car, so you are trying to find an employer on the bus route.

What if...there is someone who lives close to me who has reliable transportation and that person's employer is hiring? What if I haven't even met this person yet, but I could start looking?

What if...I got a new job that paid me enough to get a reliable vehicle? Then I could look for work outside the bus route.

What if...I could find someone to loan me a car or taxi fare until I got paid?

What if...I ask my friends who drive to work if they might carpool with me, and let me take my turns driving after I have been working long enough to get a vehicle?

What if...I know five people who would each agree to drive me one day a week to work if I pay the cost of gas?

What if...I take a job on the bus route now, even one I don't like, but I start saving right away to buy a vehicle?

What if...my place of worship knows someone who doesn't drive much, and could possibly loan me a vehicle during the week?

Maybe you feel you are limited geographically to a particular region. Perhaps you own your house and the real estate market is slow. Or you have family members who don't want to move, or a relative you care for. Perhaps you feel limited in how far away you can look for a new job.

What if...there is a great job waiting for me outside the area where I've been looking?

What if...I decided it was okay to look outside the city/region where I live now?

What if...this new company would help with moving expenses?

What if...this new community would be better for my family than where I live now? Maybe we just don't know it yet! Maybe we fear something that would actually be better for us.

What if...my mother would be happier in a new area, and she doesn't know it yet? Maybe there are some great places that will offer more activities and support and help her make new friends? She might enjoy people who want to hear her stories and haven't heard them a thousand times already. She might like a new minister and a new church. What if she ended up really happy that we made the move?

What if...I really like it here, but there are other places I might like even better?

Perhaps you have a specific set of skills, or have held a consistent job title in the past, and you just aren't finding much, if anything, that is a match to your past experience.

What if...I tried looking in some new fields for job postings, instead of the ones I usually search?

What if...I found another field that could use someone with my experience?

What if...I found a job in another area that paid better than I was earning before?

What if...I found a completely new career field I never considered before and I really loved it?

What if...I open myself to new job possibilities, and try on some new career hats, so to speak, to see if there are great jobs out there for me I never knew existed before?

What if...I didn't limit my search so much? What if...I expanded my search? What if...I stopped trying to weed out the postings and actually browsed all of them? What if...I talked to my friends in all fields, and asked them for ideas?

Be open to trying new things. Be open to applying for jobs you haven't considered before. Release yourself from limitations and see what happens.

What If-ing Beliefs That Were Getting in My Way

1) A concern I have about a possible limitation:

What if…

What if….

What if…

What if…

2) A concern I have about a possible limitation:

What if…

What if….

What if…

What if…

3) A concern I have about a possible limitation:

What if…

What if….

What if…

What if…

4) A concern I have about a possible limitation:

What if…

What if….

What if…

What if…

Change Your Clothes, Change Your Attitude

What happens to many people who are unemployed for a length of time is that their attire gradually becomes more casual. Whatever you have worn to work in the past is the equivalent of your work uniform, even if it is a business suit. The clothes that people wear when unemployed tend to be different than what they wear when working.

Some people, particularly those struggling with, or against, depression, may gain or lose weight. They may start wearing clothes that don't fit particularly well. Or they get up one day and put on the same clothes they were wearing the day before. They stop cleaning up as much before they leave the house and go out in public. It can be easy to care less about what you are wearing if you feel the world is not caring as much about you. When getting out of bed feels like a struggle, and bathing seems like something that could be postponed a day, you're in trouble.

As money gets tight over a period of prolonged unemployment, we stop spending money on our appearance. Food, obviously, takes priority over clothing. If you are supporting a family, what the kids need usually takes precedence over your needs

The reality is that when we dress up for work, we are giving ourselves a message that our appearance matters. Our clothes support our feeling that we have a place to go and something to do that is important. When we are no longer being paid for our time and what we wear doesn't seem to matter to others, we may stop caring as much.

There are several very practical steps to take here, to help shift your attitude.

1) Start dressing up again, even if you have "no place to go." Create a place to go. Get dressed and go out in public. Even if you are just going to the grocery store or public library, get out in the world again. Get dressed in your work clothes *at least* one day a week. Many people find it better to dress up five days a week, or on the same schedule they did when working. We feel and act differently when we are in work clothes. People see us differently, too. Get back in the habit of dressing for work, and for success.

2) Make sure your clothes fit. If you have gained or lost weight, find clothes that fit properly. We all feel better when we are wearing clothes that fit us.

3) Find ways to add to your wardrobe. Get new-to-you clothes by visiting local thrift stores. Go to garage and yard sales. See if you can swap clothes with a friend. Have a swap party with friends about your size, or friends who used to be your size and have gained/lost weight. Arrange a swap event at a community center or place of worship. If you need "new" business attire, see if *Dress for Success* (or an equivalent organization) exists in your community.

4) Restyle clothes already in your closet to give them a new, updated look. Swap accessories with friends, or make some inexpensive finds.

5) If you've gained or lost weight, stop beating yourself up about it. People can look good at any size. It's very common for people to get depressed, gain weight, get more depressed about the weight gain, and gain some more. (For some

people, the result is weight loss instead of gain.) What's most important right now is that you stop feeling bad about your size and figure out how to feel better about where you are.

6) If you don't know what you would wear to an interview, start thinking and planning. Find the clothes you would wear. If interview clothes are already in your closet, have you tried them on recently? Make sure they are clean and still fit well. Get dressed like you are preparing for an interview. Eventually, you will be. If you have been out of work for a long time, check to be sure your interview clothes are still current in style and appropriateness. Even if you have been out of work for years, the interviewer will be evaluating your appearance based on current standards of attire, not on what you wore to your last job.

7) If you are trying to enter a new field or you are interviewing for your first job, you need to evaluate what is appropriate interview attire for the position you want, then dress for that job. Be seen publicly. Get comfortable wearing those clothes. If you are not used to wearing a suit, for instance, and you aspire to a job that would require wearing one, you don't want to seem uncomfortable in a suit at an interview. Wear it enough in public that you feel "at home" in it.

8) If you have not been actively networking, start again, and be wearing professional attire when you do. You should be seen in attire that is a match to the position you are seeking, not to your unemployed status. When people see you, they need to be thinking of the assets you can provide a

company. Visual reminders are important. Word-of-mouth is still a common way to find job referrals and recommendations.

Ten Little Things

Sometimes we just need to feel better – soon! Maybe your mind is in a spiral of negative thinking and you need to interrupt it. Maybe you just got some bad news. Maybe you woke up with a pessimistic attitude. It helps to have a plan, in advance, about how to DO something to make yourself feel better. Nothing helps us feel better quickly than doing something that engages us and gives us a new focus.

Make a list of ten (or more) little, or minor, things you can do to feel better. Each of these should be something you can complete in a half hour or so – or even less. If you are having a rough day or a rough few minutes, you can pull this list out and pick something from it. Make sure there is variety: what you may want to do can vary depending on how you feel. Here are some examples, in first person, as if you were writing them on your list:

- ➢ Take a walk.
- ➢ Clean off a table or counter.
- ➢ Replace burned-out light bulbs.
- ➢ Replace dead batteries.
- ➢ Spend a half-hour going through the closet, and donate to a local thrift store or shelter.
- ➢ Go through an overcrowded drawer and pull out what isn't needed or used. Give it away, discard it, or find it a new home.
- ➢ Clean out the medicine cabinet.
- ➢ Call a friend I haven't talked to in a while. (The call should feel uplifting or distracting to you, or don't do it.)

- ➢ Check the dates on canned food in the pantry or refrigerator, throwing out expired products.
- ➢ Wipe the shelves in the refrigerator.
- ➢ Clean out the oven or microwave.
- ➢ Assemble the _____ that I bought that is still sitting in the box.
- ➢ Help a neighbor/friend with a project.
- ➢ Write a letter, card, text or e-mail to someone I care about.
- ➢ Put on some music and dance.
- ➢ Make a list of my favorite songs and start singing!
- ➢ Play a musical instrument – or start learning one!
- ➢ Find some happy/funny/inspiring videos to watch on *YouTube*.
- ➢ Go through a stack of mail, magazines, or newspapers, then sort and recycle.
- ➢ Offer to mow a neighbor's lawn, shovel snow, trim their bushes, weed the garden, or "just do it" for an elderly, sick or busy neighbor.
- ➢ Start to learn a new language—or review one already learned. (*YouTube* is full of free language lessons, many lasting only a few minutes.)
- ➢ If I have been putting off any yard work or project of my own, then spend a half-hour getting started.
- ➢ Is it trash day? After the trash has been picked up, put the lids on neighbors' trash bins, or take trash totes up by their garages (or where stored). (If it's raining or snowing and they come home to find lids on, they will be nicely surprised and appreciate the kindness.)

- ➢ Play! Play a game, a puzzle, shoot baskets – whatever is fun. (If there is anyone else home to play with, even better!)
- ➢ Find someone to be nice to. Smile when it is not expected. Say something cheerful to everyone I encounter. Get out for a half-hour with the specific intention of being friendly to everyone I meet. I will try to uplift others. (I won't let it bother me if they don't reciprocate: it is my job to try to cheer others. If they don't appreciate it, that's okay; their attitude has nothing to do with me.)
- ➢ Go to a store and look for opportunities to help people. I can reach an item for someone who is trying to get a product but not able to. I can get a shopping cart or basket for someone with too many items to carry. I can load groceries into a car for a person who is handicapped. I can make cheerful remarks to a salesclerk having a bad day. So I don't seem intrusive, I can ask before I do it, "May I help you with that?" I don't have to have a job to be useful, helpful and appreciated by others.

Ten Little Things I Can Do to Feel Better…

1)

2)

3)

4)

5)

6)

7)

8)

9)

10)

And More:

11)

12)

13)

14)

15)

16)

17)

18)

19)

20)

Opportunities Unemployment Has Brought

How you present a period of unemployment to a potential employer, and how you think of it yourself, can be very important to its ending. Try to think about some of the advantages, not the disadvantages, that this time has brought you. Make a list. What are some opportunities you have had as a result of being unemployed?

Here are some examples. See if any of them fit, then make a list of your own. Include examples below if they are applicable. You might also get ideas to implement if you are going through a period of unemployment now.

➢ I have had time to examine who I am and where I am in my life. I have done an honest assessment of my strengths and weaknesses, and I know the direction I want to move my life in. This time has helped me gain great clarity, focus, and drive.

➢ I had time to think about why I lost my last job, and how I can prevent that from happening again.

➢ I have been able to spend more time with my family, friends or neighbors and now know them better.

➢ I have a great spouse, and the period of unemployment gave me time to be more helpful at home.

➢ I took up a hobby I have always wanted to start.

- ➢ I got projects around home done that I'd wanted to finish for a long time.

- ➢ I couldn't use lack of time anymore as an excuse not to exercise, so I got in shape.

- ➢ I had time to learn a new language.

- ➢ I had time to do some/more volunteer work.

- ➢ I did an internship in a work area I have always wanted to explore.

- ➢ I got more involved in the community/local schools/my house of worship.

- ➢ I realized how resourceful and creative I can be when I need to stretch my dollars.

- ➢ I found out I'm more resilient than I thought.

- ➢ I learned to shop less and do more with what I already have.

- ➢ I found that I have some wonderfully supportive people in my life.

- ➢ I developed greater appreciation for what I already have in my life.

Advantages and Opportunities:
Benefits I Have Gained While Finding New Employment

1)

2)

3)

4)

5)

6)

7)

8)

9)

10)

11)

12)

13)

14)

15)

What Are You Good At?

Going through a period of unemployment can cause us to question our self-esteem and self-worth. So let's consider: *what are you good at?*

If you have been employed before, make a list of skills you developed at your previous employer(s).

If you have volunteered before, make a list of skills from that experience.

If you do not have any work experience but were recently a student, use that as your point of reference in listing your skills.

If you are a homemaker, or have been working at home since you have been unemployed, list those skills.

That is step one. The second step is to take the skills and, if necessary, translate them into qualities an employer might find beneficial. Here are some examples.

Maybe you have been busy driving kids to and from school and to their after-school activities. So you put down, *I am a good chauffeur.*

Then let's look at it from a marketable, job-skills perspective. Being a good chauffeur means you have effective time-management skills. You have to plan ahead to know how long a drive will take. You have to know how to "lead" the kids into the car and "manage" them while they are there.

Cooking dinner for a family can require organizational, time-management, and budget skills. You have to plan, make sure the meal is affordable, purchase or organize your ingredients, and budget your time so all dishes finish at the same moment. You have to clean and organize your workplace afterward.

If you have been a student, then you learned how to manage your time, complete assignments, plan ahead, work with others, respect authority, etc.

So, while you may have specific job-related skills you have used with an employer in the past, you may discover additional skills you have not considered recently, such as time management, budget, and organizational skills.

I have heard people describe periods of unemployment as "I just stayed home." "I took care of the kids." "I took charge of my grandfather's care." *Reframe* what you have been doing. You don't want to inflate a task bigger than it is. But telling a job interviewer you discovered new depths of patience when you accompanied a kindergarten and 30 five-year-olds on their class field trip can help humanize you and lighten the interview, particularly if the interviewer is a fellow parent or grandparent.

What I Am Good At…

1) A Skill I am Good at…

And how that can benefit my new employer…

2) A Skill I am Good at…

And how that can benefit my new employer…

3) A Skill I am Good at…

And how that can benefit my new employer…

4) A Skill I am Good at…

And how that can benefit my new employer…

5) A Skill I am Good at...

And how that can benefit my new employer...

6) A Skill I am Good at...

And how that can benefit my new employer...

7) A Skill I am Good at...

And how that can benefit my new employer...

8) A Skill I am Good at...

And how that can benefit my new employer...

Talents

While skills are abilities usually considered to have developed from knowledge, training, or practice, talents are natural abilities or aptitudes that often seem innate to who we are. Sometimes they are developed and enhanced over a period of time. For instance, someone may have a natural talent or affinity for music, but learns through dedicated years of practice how to play a musical instrument well. A person may have a special ability to work with food, and decides to become a chef. A future athlete may have seemed athletically inclined even as a child. What natural talents do you have? What have you always found yourself drawn to? We *all* have special talents, even if no one else has recognized them.

Think about activities you were interested in as a child or teenager. Were there areas of curiosity, or activities you were particularly good at? For instance, some people are marvelous storytellers. Others are astute listeners. Some find ways to get along with everyone. Other people are great conversationalists, keen observers, or wonderful entertainers. Some folks are very comfortable leading groups of people. Public speaking or writing comes easily for some and can be frightening to others.

What are your special talents?

If your closest friends made a list of your talents and positive qualities, how would they describe you?

Are there talents and interests you haven't shared with anyone, because you are afraid of being ridiculed? Or perhaps you were taught this was "just not practical" as a way to make a living.

There is no time like a period of unemployment to explore new interests. Maybe talents you have placed on the back burner need to be moved forward. Perhaps they hold the keys to new opportunities, new careers. Or developing them while you are unemployed may lift your spirits and rejuvenate you. If they've been hidden and starving for a long time: feed them!

This is a great time to recognize your talents, nurture them, and appreciate them. They are part of what makes *you* the wonderful and unique person you are.

My Talents, Natural Abilities and Interests Include…

Talents, Natural Abilities and Interests
I Might Want to Explore/Grow Are …

Why I Am a Great Employee!

This list is obvious from the title: when you are hired, what will you be able to offer a company/organization? Look for items to put on this list that are in addition to the previous lists of talents and skills.

Make a list of at least ten items. This is particularly helpful to review before an interview.

Address your list to your future employer.

Here are some examples. Keep in mind that the items on your list may vary according to the type of job for which you are applying.

I am a GREAT EMPLOYEE because...

➢ I am reliable. You can count on me to show up on time and work my assigned schedule.

➢ I am prompt.

➢ I like to be helpful. I like to jump in on projects and assist others when I can be of value.

➢ I will get any job you assign me completed on time.

➢ I work well without supervision.

➢ I can be a leader when appropriate, but I also enjoy being a team player.

- ➢ I recognize that what is important is getting the project completed successfully; it doesn't matter who gets credit.

- ➢ I have lots of prior work experience in this field.

- ➢ I have taken courses specific to success in this industry.

- ➢ I know how to be tactful when dealing with others.

- ➢ I am a quick learner. I can easily learn any skill I apply myself to.

- ➢ I have experience in _____.

- ➢ I have skills from other work/volunteer experience that is applicable to this position, even though this job is a new field to me. Some of those skills are

  _____.

- ➢ I really want to succeed. And I want you to be glad you hired me. I want you to feel really good six months from now, a year from now, because you saw my commitment, drive and ability to benefit this company.

I Am a Great Employee Who Will Benefit Your Business Because…

1)

2)

3)

4)

5)

6)

7)

8)

9)

10)

11)

12)

13)

14)

15)

Before the Interview: Finding Positive Qualities

Any employment advisor will tell you that you should research a company before your interview. In fact, if the position requires a cover letter, you should begin your research before writing the letter.

However, if there is a job or field you are interested in, you would do well to start researching *now*: don't wait until the interview.

Remember that interviews can be scheduled weeks in advance. *Or* you might be called in the morning and asked if you are free that afternoon. Don't expect time to prepare. Prepare now.

Keep in mind that some companies will not allow much lead time simply to see how well prepared you really are for a position with their firm.

You need to familiarize yourself with the specific company *and* the type of business you want to work in. Your research needs to extend beyond the company itself to the type of work you want to do.

For example, if you want to work in a retail business selling antiques, you should be researching antiques as well as the business of selling.

If you want to work in a company manufacturing automobiles, research the company and that type of automobile. You may also want to research the current process of manufacturing, and tasks that might be related to the specific job you have applied for.

If you want a clerical position but have been out of the job market for a while, make sure you are researching ways to prepare documents using current software. Do you know the type of computers and programs used by the company where you are applying? It's okay to call and ask. If it is different software than you are used to, check with friends to see if any have it on their home computers or see if it's readily available online. Also contact libraries and local colleges/universities to see what is available free to the public. Temporary employment agencies may offer free training to help you gain skills that you can use on a temporary assignment; then you can list that as experience when applying to a future permanent employer. Some places of worship will let their members use their office computers to get ready for a new job.

You need to become familiar with the language, terminology, and acronyms used in the area to which you are applying. You want it apparent to an interviewer that you are comfortable with the language discussed. Your preparation may also help you ask better questions. And, particularly if you are starting a new field of work, it may help you assess if this is really the job for you.

As you become comfortable with the business and type of work you desire -- particularly if it is new or you are updating your skills -- you may uncover other employment possibilities, job listings, and networking opportunities. I have known people who could not "get in the door" to a company where they wanted to work. Then they did something "new" such as volunteer work, and connected with someone who helped open that door. Or they took a temporary position to gain entry to the company and eventually were hired permanently. Sometimes we stop expecting doors to open. As the old saying goes, we need to forget the closed door and look for an open window.

As you are researching the company, it can be helpful to write down a list of positive qualities about that employer. What are aspects of this organization that resonate positively with you? If all you have is, "They provide a paycheck," *try harder*. What do you like about this company? What are you discovering about the company that is a pleasant surprise? Did you know how the company started? How do you think their employees feel about working there, or do you know anyone working there? What positive qualities would current employees find? How would you feel about saying to your friends and family that you have a job there? Where do you see this company going in the future? If you were to project the need for their area of business or specialization ten or twenty years into the future, what do you see?

It is important to have a positive view of a company you want to be your future employer. This can be a helpful exercise to practice before you write a cover letter. But it is essential before an interview. Even if you don't have an opportunity to share what you know during an interview, you will feel better prepared and will approach the interview more positively. If you don't get that position, you will still have gained more experience finding positive aspects of a future employer. If you interview with a competitor of that company in the future, they may be impressed at how knowledgeable you are about their competition and why you find their organization preferable. If an interviewer asks, "Why do you want to work for this company?" then you will have an enthusiastic response.

A Sample List: Positive Qualities of This Employer
(write this out on a separate piece of paper for positions
you are really interested in and/or before an interview)

1) Aspects of this Company/Organization I Like:

2) Reasons I Would Feel Proud/Pleased to Work Here:

3) Aspects I Like of the Way this Organization Started, and/or How They Do Business Today:

4) Things I Discovered about this Company in my Research that Were Pleasant Surprises:

5) What I Like About this Organization's Future:

6) Why I Want to Work for this Company:

Telling a Different Story...

Many people have *past-itis* and *present-itis*. These are conditions of thought. We give our attention to what was and what is. We focus on what we don't like about those periods of time, instead of giving our attention to what is going to be, to what we want to create in our lives. What do you want in your future?

When you meet someone on the street and they ask you how the job search is going, what do you say? When someone asks how you are doing and that person wants a genuine answer, how do you respond?

Most of us habitually answer these kinds of questions according to what we are experiencing at the present moment. And if we want a job and don't have one yet, that answer may not feel very good to us.

In fact, people who are unemployed often DREAD these kinds of questions. *Please don't ask me*, we are silently saying. Or we walk in another direction to avoid running into the potential questioner.

So... plan ahead and come up with a different story. A better story.

You have some practice now in learning to look at reality differently. Still truthful. But perhaps differently than you have in the past.

What kind of story could you tell about your present and future that would feel good to you? What story would also feel true?

Let's consider some examples, then you can work on developing your own. It is a good idea to come up with three or four responses that feel good to you. Then practice them so they become your "automatic" responses when you are asked. If you have been focusing on your successes and your skills, you may be feeling better already. You may even feel hopeful.

How are you doing?

Great. It's been wonderful to have time to catch up on projects and consider new career opportunities.

How are you feeling?

Hopeful. Optimistic. There are some great opportunities out there. I have some wonderful leads. Life is turning around for me. I can feel it.

Have you gotten a job yet?

Well, my jobs may not be the traditional kind right now. I am working out of my home, taking care of the kids, trying to help my spouse feel supported. I'm busier than I've ever been, getting a lot accomplished. I'm really taking advantage of this time to catch up on projects, reading, research. It's been a great time for building relationships with my family, and I've been lucky to enjoy it.

Are you still unemployed?

I may not have a job with a paycheck yet, but I will soon. I'm working as hard as I ever have. You might say I'm employing myself, or my family is employing me.

What's new?

New jobs, new opportunities, new interests. I'm doing some volunteer work, researching new career paths. My life is getting ready to take off in a new direction, and it feels wonderful.

Work on telling a different story, a better story. How do you want your future to look? Aside from the employment picture, are there other avenues you can pursue to create what you desire? If you have hobby materials tucked away in a box or closet, get them out and rekindle your interest. If you felt like you never had time to attend your kids' or grandkids' games or events, now you can become their biggest fan. Maybe it's time to learn a new language or join a local organization or book club. Is there a place in your community where you have wanted to volunteer? If you don't cook at home because you don't know how, learn now and surprise your spouse or friends.

Everyone you meet is a potential connection to that new job. If you seem depressed and hopeless, people may feel sorry for you, but they may also keep their distance. If they are impressed with your attitude and your resilience, they will be impressed with you. And if they share that impression of your resilience with someone who might become a potential employer, so much the better!

It is important when we don't feel good about our present to change the way we are looking at it. A new perspective can have far greater impact than merely changing the words we say.

Look at the future, not the past. Even in this present moment, look at the future if the present is not pleasing. Give your attention to what you want to create.

Crafting My New Story:
Answers that reflect the future I am creating

How I am doing…

How I am feeling…

How I am/my family is benefitting from my time…

How I am employing myself…

How I am finding ways to be positive and optimistic…

What's new in my life that I feel good about…

My Success Journal

We often have lists running mentally of what is not going well in our lives and what we would like to be different. The success journal is a deliberate effort to focus on what is going *right*. Take a notebook and dedicate it to this purpose, or establish a new file on your computer, phone, or tablet. At the beginning of the journal, make a list of significant successes you have had in your life. Leave several pages blank so you can add to it over time. Then start a new section where you make daily entries. Every day, write down your most significant success of the day, or write down as much as you want from the day that you would consider successful. It doesn't matter if anyone else views this as a success: this is your world, your perspective.

If you want to post successes related to job-finding, you might list events such as:

➢ Found a great job to apply for

➢ Researched the company

➢ Completed two new applications

➢ Discovered new opportunity to network this Thursday

➢ Developed great opening paragraph for cover letter

➢ Heard about new job opening from Marty

➢ Took my interview suit to the dry cleaner so it's ready

➢ Finished testing for application made yesterday

➢ Made follow-up phone call about last week's interview

➢ Wrote thank you e-mails to two people who forwarded me job listings

➢ Practiced answering interview questions aloud in mirror

➢ Made list of accomplishments at previous employers.

But we also have many successes in our lives that are not job-related, and we would still benefit from reinforcing:

➢ Got the kids to school on time

➢ Convinced Joey to wear "real clothes" to school and not the pajamas he was insisting on

➢ Completed grocery shopping within budget

➢ Got the cupcakes finished for tomorrow's bake sale

➢ Finished the week's laundry

➢ Returned all phone calls

➢ Had a great walk with the dog

➢ Ran all my errands and made it home on schedule

➢ The kids finished their homework *before* supper.

Only you know what feels like a success *to you*. But successes always *feel good*. Someone who has been deeply depressed might list getting out of bed or taking a shower as a success. Been putting the same clothes on day after day? Then intentionally putting on a different outfit would be a success. Been grumpy? Then choosing to leave the house a few minutes early to avoid arguing with a mate could be a success. Walking around the block to blow off steam instead of yelling back could be a genuine accomplishment. Not been moving or exercising much? Then going to the mall on a rainy or snowy day to walk got you out of your home and moving.

You have to list what was successful *for you* in your day. Don't give in to the tendency to talk about the problem that led to the solution. Don't feel sorry for yourself because you had a problem. Keep your focus on the solution. Pay attention to *what you did that was solution-oriented,* not problem-oriented. Every item on your success list should feel good to you.

My Successes Today

Successes I Am Experiencing Now...

Sample Topics for a Daily Success Journal:

Today's Successes Include...

A Significant Success Today Was...

A Job-Finding Process Success Today Was...

A Personal Success or Accomplishment Today Was...

Something I Did Today that was Solution-Oriented...

My Success Lunch

You have probably heard of the concept of the "power lunch." The success lunch is similar. You gather with a friend or fellow job-finder(s) for a meal or for tea or coffee. The intention is to gather for an hour to focus only on the positive aspects of your lives. No negative or pessimistic talk is allowed. This gives each of you an opportunity to practice and further develop your success consciousness.

Develop a list of questions at the beginning. You may want to take exercises from this book and practice them with each other. You might meet once, or decide to meet weekly. You might decide to text each other daily. This is about practicing how to think and talk *success*. Ideas for topics include:

- ➢ Successes in my life
- ➢ My dream for the future
- ➢ What I want in my life someday; why I want it; how I will feel when I have it
- ➢ Entries from my success journal this past week.

The people involved should agree to a few ground rules:

1) Only positive talk allowed.
2) No judgments. Do not judge yourself or others.
3) Don't discredit what someone else considers a success; success is personal.
4) Don't talk over each other, or talk at the same time. Allow the speaker to finish.

5) Each participant should spend about the same amount of time talking.
6) If you are going to say anything about what someone else has shared, it should be brief and uplifting.
7) No advice unless someone specifically asks for a piece of information.

The point here is to give you an opportunity to practice talking successfully. This is not about creating a support group. This is a practice group: to practice thinking and talking *success*.

If you have a large group and some people talk significantly more than others, develop a timing system. For instance, each person has five minutes to share, or whatever the group decides. You can use a timer, select a timekeeper, or simply have each person serve as timekeeper for the next person after he/she speaks.

Another suggestion to consider is to have a neutral item in the center of the table or group, such as wrapped candies or mints or even paperclips. If someone starts speaking negatively or becomes problem-oriented, you simply take a neutral object and lay it down in front of him/her or hand it to the person. The hint is obvious. You can also do this if someone begins to offer a negative judgment of another person's success or situation. It is a gentle way of reminding the person to become more intentional and mindful about what he or she is saying. Sometimes we speak faster than we consciously think, and we need to pause and pay attention to what we are actually saying.

If you do this over a period of time, you may find you need to begin with shorter meetings. It can take people a while to become comfortable talking about their successes as well as recognizing and remembering them. If you are meeting a friend for coffee, you might begin with a couple of successes and take turns. Sometimes, when one person shares, it will remind you of something else you can talk about when it is your turn again.

It is important to recognize this is practice: this is not bragging. This is not about "one-upping" other members of the group. It is also vital to realize that everyone may be at different places on their journeys. Someone who was suddenly laid off two weeks ago may be in a very different space than a person who had two interviews earlier in the week. You don't want to compare your successes to anyone else's, or use the group as a chance to "beat yourself up." The measure of success in this group is not the content shared, but the time you spend practicing as you talk and think about success.

Changing the Recordings

We all have "thought recordings" we play and replay in our minds. These are usually statements we carry internally for years. Often, they had their origins in childhood or previous relationships. Parents or teachers may have pronounced negative sentences on us and we remembered them. Maybe we were criticized at earlier jobs. Perhaps we had relationship partners who thought we didn't measure up to their expectations. Somehow, somewhere, most of us hear critical, negative statements and then repeat them. They become internal mantras we often perpetuate for years. It is important to identify these statements, and then change them.

How do we identify them? Easy. We think them and they don't feel good.

They don't feel good when we *think* them. *They don't feel good* when we *hear* them.

It doesn't matter if you think there is some truth to the statement. Often, these statements resonate with us because we think there might be some truth to them, we fear there might be some truth, or they come from someone to whom we assign meaning and power in our lives. If a total stranger walked up to you on the street and said something negative, it would seem odd, but you probably wouldn't replay it for years. If a teacher or parent or someone you respect and love makes the same statement to you, it can hold an entirely different kind of power.

We often use these statements to beat ourselves up, from the inside. When we are feeling down or low in our lives, we repeat these statements to ourselves even more.

Some people will take statements like these and turn them upside down. A teacher tells a student she is stupid and will never amount to anything. But instead of believing it, the student decides to show the teacher and work really heard, becoming an academic star. A coach tells a young player he isn't athletic and should give up sports. The young player dedicates himself to the game and eventually becomes a professional athlete. We've all heard these stories.

Many of us, however, don't turn the statement upside down. Many of us repeat it and believe it. Many of us repeat these statements for years. Even if it wasn't true *at all* in the beginning, we believe it to be true, or worry it is, as time passes.

It is crucial to change the recordings in your mind if they are negative. *If they are negative, they are not serving you.*

Negative statements are rarely of value. Negative statements rarely improve someone, and never uplift a person's spirits.

Negative statements diminish and dehumanize. What is really amazing is that the first time we heard those words, we *felt* them try to diminish us. Yet now, we are the ones who keep repeating them.

Sometimes, it is like listening to a station on television that we did not choose, to programs we don't like and wouldn't want to watch. But that's what was on the television when we walked in the room, so that's what we listen to. Except this is your mind. This is your room. That's your television playing. If you don't like the channel, change it!

Make a list of the negative statements you unconsciously repeat. Then turn them upside down. Find evidence to argue with that statement and prove it is *not true*. And then replace the old statement with the new.

Old statement: You're so lazy.

The Real Evidence: I have worked really hard much of my life. If there's a job to be done, I get it finished. And if I like doing something, I work even harder. Hard work is enjoyable when it's doing something I care about. I like the sense of accomplishment. Hard work can feel really good.

New statement: I am a really hard worker, especially when it's something I care about.

Old statement: You're such a procrastinator. You never finish anything you start.

The Real Evidence: I finish tasks all the time. But there's a difference between doing what feels good and keeps my attention, and doing tasks I feel I should but don't care as much about. Sometimes I am enthusiastic about a task, but my interest wanes when I start because it isn't as interesting as I expected. I mostly procrastinate about tasks that are "shoulds" and not necessarily what I want to do. Still, there are many tasks I finish simply because they have to be done. When a task is important to me or necessary, I get it done.

New statement: I am a very responsible person.
I complete any task I set my mind to.

Old statement: You're so fat. No one is going to hire somebody that fat.

The Real Evidence: Well, I may be overweight, but there are many people in the world heavier than I am. And my size has nothing to do with my ability to perform most jobs. I know

I overeat when I am stressed, and not having a job has been really stressful. I haven't been heavy my entire life. I was a "normal" weight once. Maybe I am heavier right now, but that doesn't define me as a person. It doesn't define the value I can provide to a company. I really see this as a temporary situation. And if it isn't, well, that's my choice. I know the more I see myself as fat and think others do, the fatter I seem to become. It doesn't help me at all to think this way, or apply that label to myself. If people took the time to get to know me, they would discover the real me. In fact, if an interviewer wants to judge me based strictly on my size, then that person is going to miss out on a great employee. I have a lot of skill to offer an employer. And I would be a very loyal employee. Weights are flexible. They go up and down. My size isn't permanent. It's just an indicator of where my body is today. The people who matter to me will always know the real me, and not stop at superficial judgments. Sizes change. I change. My weight is only a temporary indicator of where my body is today.

New statement: Who I *really am* is *fabulous*. My generous size reflects my generous nature. I can feel good about who I am at any size. I can dress attractively at any size. I can get a wonderful job at any size. I can easily live with myself because *I know how great I am*. I love and accept who I am in this moment.

The next time you start to replay an old message, *stop yourself.* You can intentionally interrupt your thinking and tell yourself: *that's the old message*. Then ask yourself: *what's the new message?* Say the new message to yourself. Then repeat it. And repeat it again.

Do this often enough, and the old statement will fade away. The new statement will become your habit. This takes practice, but it is worth it. *Reclaim your mind and your power!* Let the statements you make to yourself be intentional and beneficial.

Developing New Thought Recordings

Old statement #1 (that is critical, and not helpful to me to keep thinking):

But the real evidence on this topic is:

So my new thought on this topic is:

Old statement #2 (that is critical, and not helpful to me to keep thinking):

But the real evidence on this topic is:

So my new thought on this topic is:

Old statement #3 (that is critical, and not helpful to me to keep thinking):

But the real evidence on this topic is:

So my new thought on this topic is:

Old statement #4 (that is critical, and not helpful to me to keep thinking):

But the real evidence on this topic is:

So my new thought on this topic

What is Your Theme Song?

If you don't already have one, pick a theme song for this next phase of your life. Is there a piece of music that really resonates with you? That you find empowering? There may be a song that immediately jumps into your mind. If not, there are many choices available. Find one that works for you. I am not recommending any of the titles that follow: you have to find your own. And many of these songs have been recorded by multiple artists. But, just to start you thinking, here are some popular selections that listeners have found inspirational. A favorite for many is the *Theme from Rocky*: *Gonna Fly Now, Flying High Now*, Bon Jovi's *It's My Life*, the theme from *Chariots of Fire,* or *Impossible Dream*. Others like *I Have Confidence* or *Climb Every Mountain* from *The Sound of Music*, or *I Am Woman, Hear Me Roar* that was revived in *Sex and the City 2*.

Maybe you find *Circle of Life* from *The Lion King* inspiring, Michael Jackson's *Heal the World, Somewhere Over the Rainbow, I'm Walking on Sunshine,* or Louis Armstrong's *What a Wonderful World*. Maybe your theme song is Lady Gaga's *Born This Way*, Cyndi Lauper's *True Colors*, or Enigma's *Return to Innocence*. Other music that might resonate is *You Raise Me Up, When You Believe, I Believe I Can Fly, Music of My Heart, Reach, Win,* and *Hero.* There may be religious music that inspires you: *Amazing Grace*, for instance, has touched many. Or maybe you have written your own theme song.

One suggestion to incorporate easy inspiration and new affirmations into your life is to take a song you like, even a children's song, and rewrite the lyrics using phrases you need to remind yourself, that can uplift you.

Make sure you pick or write a theme song that inspires and encourages you. You should feel better when you listen to it: it should lift your spirits. Put the music in multiple places, so it is easily accessible when you need to hear it. Sometimes music can uplift us in ways that words alone cannot.

My Theme Song Is…

General Statements of Well-Being

It is very helpful to have some general statements of positive belief that you carry with you at all times. These need to be default statements that you can bring forward in your thoughts whenever needed.

You might bring your statements forward when you are anxious or worried. If you catch yourself saying something internally that is not of value to you, reach for your general statements of well-being.

These statements must feel true to you: they must resonate with you and your beliefs.

For instance, you might believe: *Everything is always working out for me.* You may not know how or when. But you know that you have had hard times before, and you have always made it through.

I know it is going to be all right. Again, you don't need the particulars of how it is going to work out. But you have been in struggles before, and always come through on the other side. Here are some other examples:

Something good comes out of everything.
Only good is ahead for me.
Light always follows darkness.
My life is getting better and better.
I can really feel that good things are happening for me.
My life is moving in a positive direction.
I know my future is bright, and my present is getting brighter.
It will be okay. In fact, I am okay right now, in this moment.
Well-being is everywhere.

Avoid cliché statements that you don't believe. For instance, some people might find comfort in the idea that the brightest rainbows follow the darkest storms. Other people might consider the idea romantic or sentimental. You need to find a statement that fits you.

If you are a religious person, you may find a helpful statement in a religious text. Millions of people, for instance, have found comfort in the Bible's Twenty-third Psalm.

You want your statements to feel true, but also hopeful. You need a statement that will reassure you when you feel stressed.

Sometimes, it can be hard to feel that well-being has dominated most of our lives. But most people experience more positive, or at least neutral, than negative in their lives. Even during the bleakest of times, we can find positive things if we look for them. Find a statement that reasserts your well-being, and let it become your new mantra.

My Statements of Well-Being Include:

Positive Qualities of Past Jobs and Employers

Often, we look to our past experiences to help us define what we want in the future. We know what we liked in past work environments, for example. We hope to find these positive qualities with a future employer. For instance, if I had an office with great windows that let in lots of light, I may hope for another office that is bright with good views.

But what we did not like can help us clarify what we want in the future, too. If I worked in a factory with no windows and felt isolated from outside light and weather, it may be important to me to find a job with windows that allow natural light. I discovered that light is important to me.

A productive exercise is to remember aspects of previous employers that you liked. Think about your most recent job. Start making lists of qualities you appreciated.

For example:
- "I liked the way my ideas were respected at my old job."
- "I appreciated how accessible the management was."
- "I valued the variety of food in the break room. It was convenient, good, and cheap."

If there were aspects you did not like, what did it clarify for you that you do want at your next job? Keep the focus on what you want, not on what you don't. For example, "My next job will have big windows that allow lots of light."

What were some positive aspects of the work environment? Reach as far as you can for qualities that you appreciated then, or value now. Perhaps the atmosphere was quiet and calm, or maybe it was noisy and alive with activity. Perhaps you liked working alone, or enjoyed the camaraderie of teamwork. Did you have the tools necessary to do your work? What tools did you most appreciate? Was the workplace easily accessible? Was it a short commute with nearby parking, or was the location close to public transportation? Perhaps there were good restaurants nearby. What was positive about the location?

What were some positive qualities of your boss/supervisor? What did you like about the style of supervision? If you did not like the style of supervision, what style would you appreciate in the future? How were you treated? Who in the organization respected you and treated you well? Keep the focus on what you liked and what you want more of in your future.

What about the work itself did you value? Was it always changing and challenging? Was it routine and allowed your mind time to roam? Did you like work that allowed you freedom and creativity, or did you like tasks that were clearly defined and outlined? What about your co-workers/colleagues? What aspects did you appreciate in them?

Start the list of positive qualities about your most recent position. Then consider earlier jobs. Go back and add items over time, as you remember more characteristics you would like in a future position.

Positive Qualities of Past Workplaces

Qualities I Will Value in My New Workplace

What I Want in a New Job

This is an exercise to clarify what you want. You know you want a new job, or you wouldn't be reading this book. What do you want in a new job?

Often, if we have been on the job market a while, we get less and less selective as time (and unemployment) wears on. We start applying for (almost) anything. We lose sight of what we originally wanted and hoped for. We give up most of our aspirational thinking. We may eventually decide we'll settle for any position: we just need a paycheck.

This exercise is meant to take you back to a place of wanting and hoping. What kind of job do you want? How do you want to feel about your new job? How do you want to feel about going to work? How do you want to feel as you leave your job and come home?

Start with general statements about how you want to *feel*. Write down words and phrases that feel good to you.

➤ *I want to feel_____ about my new job.* Happy? Excited? That it is a great opportunity? That it could lead to better things?

➤ *I feel the work is_____.* What matters to you about the work? What positive statements would you make about a job you really liked? Say these statements as if you already have the job.

➤ *I like the feeling I have coming home from work, because_____.* I feel I got a lot accomplished? My time feels well spent? My work is enjoyable?

➤ *The best part of my new job is...*

➤ *What I like most about my new employer is...*

➤ *What I like about the new environment I'm working in is...*

> ➢ *What I like about my colleagues is...*
> ➢ *What I appreciate about my new boss is...*
> ➢ *What I like about my schedule is...*

Think about aspects of the new job that matter to you, and write down the positive qualities you want to find there. State them in the present tense, as if you are already experiencing them. *Feel* each statement as if it is true. Try to develop each statement so it takes you at least a minute to answer fully. For example, here is a woman talking about what she likes in her work schedule. The job itself is still to come. But she is projecting herself into the future and talking about it as if it is already true.

What I like about my schedule is that I work very predictable hours. The hours are the same Monday through Friday, and I like that because then I am free to schedule the rest of my life. I know I have evenings and weekends free, and that time is my own to do with as I please. I like having a constant schedule. It feels steady to me, and helps me feel secure. I have always liked jobs with the same schedule week to week. I think that is a big bonus in a job, to have hours you can count on like that. It also means I am paid for the same number of hours every week, so I know what to expect in my paycheck. And if I want to add in activities or even another job, I know the times I am going to be free. I can plan the schedule in my personal life months in advance if I want to. There's a lot of freedom to me in knowing that. That feels like real security to me. I like routine in my life. I like a dependable schedule I can count on, and the dependable paycheck that comes with it. I like being able to plan ahead. Yes, I really like the predictable hours of my new job.

The predictable hours this person likes may not be what someone else is seeking. Someone else may like variety in scheduling, the opportunity to work overtime or at home, or a salaried position where one works until the day's tasks are accomplished. You have to complete these statements about what you like and what is true for you. Don't include what other people have said you *should* want; only include what you actually *do* want.

Starting with general statements allows you to clarify what you want, but with flexibility. The person above is not specifying the type of work being done Monday through Friday, but how the schedule feels. There are many jobs that would provide the security this person enjoys.

Even if you don't know the type of work you want, you know some of the feelings you are seeking, and that is a good place to start. If you have not had success looking for work within your field, this exercise can also allow you to broaden your perspective. Perhaps there are jobs in other fields that could still fulfill much of what you want. The point is to gain clarity and allow doors to new opportunities the chance to open.

Qualities I Appreciate in my New Position
(Looking ahead, but feeling it now…)

How I feel about my new job…

What I like about the work at my new job…

What I like about the feeling I have coming home from work at my new position…

The best part of my new job is...

What I like most about my new employer is...

What I like about the new environment I'm working in is...

What I like about my colleagues is...

What I appreciate about my new boss is...

Align Your Thinking

Imagine a path in the woods between two points you travel often. In this analogy, one point is where you are now, and the other point, your destination, is your new job.

You travel this path mentally many times a day.

If this were an actual physical path, you would want it to be easy to travel. If there were obstacles on your path, perhaps branches that were blown down during a storm, you would remove them. You wouldn't want to keep walking around the obstacles every time you traveled this path: you would eliminate them. You would keep your path clean and your journey easy.

When we take mental journeys in thinking about a new job, we often find metaphorical "branches" blown down in the path. Sometimes, we come upon a branch and say, "Here is an obstacle. I have to turn around and go home now. I can't proceed." Instead of moving the branch, stepping over it or walking around it, we see it as a barrier to our progress. We stop moving forward.

I call these branches in our path *thought obstacles*. They are thoughts that impede our progress. Most importantly, they are thoughts *we allow* to impede our progress.

If our hope for finding a new job soon has been worn thin, or eroded altogether, little branches can seem like big ones. When we are already depressed or anxious, little branches can seem much, much bigger to us.

In this exercise, identify what thought obstacles lay between you and your new job. Then clean them up and get them out of your path.

Even big branches can be broken down into smaller pieces and removed from the path. But it is important to identify them.

Clarify Your Destination

First, clarify your destination. You know where you are. Now think about the job you are seeking, what lies ahead at your destination. What are the most important aspects of that new job? Let's identify five. The five I am using here may not match yours, so use your own.

1) *I want a job I can like and feel good about going to.*
2) *I want a job with an easy commute.*
3) *I want to be paid well.*
4) *I want to be respected by the people I work with and for.*
5) *I want work I enjoy doing, work that feels fulfilling.*

Identify Possible Thought Obstacles

Second, identify any thought obstacles you might have about those aspects. These statements often begin with words like "but" or words that *feel* like "but." Let's consider what some thought obstacles might be for these five aspects.

Examples of Thought Obstacles

➤ *I want a job I can like and feel good about going to.* But it seems impossible to find. But the only jobs I see listed are with employers I don't want to work for. But I've given up finding something I like and will take anything now.

➤ *I want a job with an easy commute*. But there aren't any places close to me I want to work at. But I know I'm going to have to make a long commute to get to any decent job. But there's so much traffic in the city and I really hate rush hour driving.

➤ *I want to be paid well*. But that seems like an impossible dream. But I'm ready to settle for almost anything right now that will pay the bills. But the good-paying jobs are already filled, and I'm looking at leftovers.

➤ *I want to be respected by the people I work with and for*. But I wasn't respected at my last job, and I don't expect I'll be respected at my next one, either. But employers don't have to respect you because they can easily replace you anytime they choose. But the types of jobs I'm applying for at this point just want bodies, and the employers don't actually care about the people they're hiring.

➤ *I want work I enjoy doing, work that feels fulfilling.* And (but) that seems really elusive to me. And (but) I don't know what that is anymore, or even what it feels like. And (but) I'll take any job just to pay the bills. I've given up on finding rewarding work.

These *but* statements are all obstacles on the path. They need to be cleaned up, because they are standing in your way.

You are expressing a desire: to get to your new job. And then you are finding lots of reasons you can't take this journey, or the journey isn't possible.

If you have ever played competitive sports, you know that your opponent will try to find ways to *get you off your game*. Your opponent wants to interfere with your thinking as well as your physical movements, and may try to "psych you out." When your opponent gets you doubting yourself or your abilities, makes you angry so you lose your focus, or makes noise that distracts you, your opponent is trying to redirect your energy.

If you *take the bait*, so to speak, then you are moving out of alignment with winning. But you have to choose to take the bait. You have to decide to let your opponent interfere with what you intend to be thinking and focusing on. Your opponent can't get inside your mind and think for you, so your opponent tries to get you to shift your own thinking.

The players who are most successful usually have great powers of concentration. They keep their minds on the goal, at what they want to succeed doing. They don't let outside distractions interfere.

If you allow yourself to focus on the obstacle instead of on your intended goal, you are interfering with your own success. You are *off your game*. You are focused on a problem, not a solution. And the more you focus on it, the bigger it will seem to become.

So you need to clean the thought obstacles off your path. Don't let them stand in the way, even mentally, of securing the job you want.

Clear Obstacles and Align Your Thinking

Third, clear away the obstacles with new thinking. Since you are the only one who controls your thoughts, you have to be the one who clears up the obstacles. Remember: this is your path. You need to keep it clean and easy to travel. So you are now going to dismantle the obstacles. You know where you want to go. You aren't going to let your own thought obstacles get in the way of you reaching your destination.

Thought Destination1: I want a job I can like and feel good about going to.

My thought obstacles were: But it seems impossible to find. But the only jobs I see listed are with employers I don't want to work for. But I've given up finding something I like and will take anything now.

My New Thinking: I know there are a lot of jobs out there that I would like. I don't even know what they all are. And I only need one job, not many. Even if there is an employer I don't like, there might still be a great department tucked within it where I could be happy. I was feeling tired and desperate from having searched so long. But there could be surprises ahead for me. A job that isn't what I think I want could lead me to a better job I will like. I guess I don't need to decide ahead of time if I will like a job; I can give it a chance and try it out. What I can decide is that I will make the best of it. I will go in with a winning attitude. I will do my best. I will look for positive aspects of the job to appreciate.

Thought Destination 2: I want a job with an easy commute.

My thought obstacles were: But there aren't any places close to me I want to work at. But I know I'm going to have to

107

make a long commute to get to any decent job. But there's so much traffic in the city, and where I live is far from the good employers.

My New Thinking: I guess there could be a job close to home that I just don't know about. There are lots of small businesses and even home-based employers now.
I remember Roger got a job with a company, and after two years most of his work was done from his home office. I have found that sometimes a commute is helpful to give me time to think. I know I can find ways to spend my time commuting that will still feel valuable to me. I guess I shouldn't let a commute decide for me whether this is a good job or not. I might find real value in the time I commute. So I will try not to judge in advance, and will give these jobs I thought were too far away a chance. You never really know how it might work out.

Thought Destination 3: I want to be paid well.

My thought obstacles were: But that seems like an impossible dream. But I'm ready to settle for almost anything right now. But the good-paying jobs are already filled, and I'm looking at leftovers.

My New Thinking: I know that the wage I start at does not have to be my wage for long. Most employers have opportunities open up that they can't see in advance. Maybe what is important right now is that I get my foot in the door, that I get a job to get inside the company. I know that companies do most of their hiring from within. Their employees usually have the first chance at new job openings. Once I get inside a company and they see what a good worker I am, I'll have a better chance at higher-paying positions. I shouldn't look at the starting pay as an obstacle to me being paid well eventually. I can still be paid well eventually. The company doesn't know yet that I'm a hard worker. They don't know how much I can be of value to them. So maybe a job at a lower salary will be okay to get started. I will just see it as a stepping-stone to something bigger and better.

Thought Destination 4: I want to be respected by the people I work with and for.

My thought obstacles were: But I wasn't respected at my last job, and I don't expect I'll be respected at my next one, either. But employers don't have to respect you because they can easily replace you anytime they choose. But the types of jobs I'm applying for at this point just want bodies, and the employers don't actually care about the people they're hiring.

My New Thinking: We tend to reap what we sow. If I plant seeds of respect, respect is more likely to grow around me. If I start this job respecting everyone I encounter, they will be more likely to treat me respectfully. If I find positive qualities about the people I meet and work with, maybe they will be more likely to see the positive qualities in me. When someone doesn't treat me well, I shouldn't assume it's about me. Maybe that person is just having a bad day, is stressed about something personal or had a fight with the spouse before work, or maybe that person's boss is being difficult. I don't really know what is going on for someone else, and I shouldn't take the way he/she treats me personally. I am just going to stay positive and keep treating him/her well, regardless. I am going to find something to like about everyone I meet. I want other people to feel I am treating them respectfully. I want people at my job to know I treat others well, no matter what position in the company they have. Everyone likes to be treated respectfully. Everyone deserves that. I won't judge people by how they treat others, or even by how they treat me. I'll remember I am not living life in their shoes, and I don't know what's going on for them. But I choose how I treat others. Every day, I can choose to treat people well.

Thought Destination 5: I want work I enjoy doing, work that feels fulfilling.

My thought obstacles were: And that seems really elusive to me. And I don't know what that is anymore, or even what it feels like. And I'll take any job just to pay the bills: I've given up on finding fulfillment.

My New Thinking: I can decide that any job I do, I am going to do well...to the best of my ability. I can make the work more interesting by figuring out how I can do it better. I can look for solutions to problems I encounter. I can see any job as offering me opportunities to better myself. I can see any job as providing opportunities to be creative, even in little ways. I can decide that what will be most fulfilling will be doing the job well. A lot of what defines fulfillment is personal, after all. Different people find different kinds of work fulfilling. If this job isn't something I thought would be fulfilling, then how can I make it be? How can I find pleasure in it? I am sure I can find value in any kind of work if I set my mind to it. I guess work that's easily done doesn't have the fun of the challenge. Besides, there are many ways to define what is fulfilling.

I know I am doing a good job, and that means a lot to me.
I know I am treating others well, and that feels good to me.
I can meet and even surpass my own standards. I like challenging myself. Personal satisfaction can be very fulfilling.

As we have discussed earlier in this book, you have to practice new thinking. When you feel a *"but"* creeping into your story of what you want, intentionally shift to your new thinking. Stop yourself, and interject the new thoughts. Be clear: *I'm not thinking that way anymore. I'm now thinking/remembering...*and then insert your new thoughts.

When you are around other people who insert *buts* into your path, don't be thrown off your game. If you are around someone who is also job-seeking and is finding lots of excuses not to be successful, avoid the temptation to sympathize and bond with this person through hardship. You can share your new story with this person and demonstrate a different way to think. *I used to think that way, too. Then I realized....*

Some people find it helpful to write their thought journeys on paper. Then they will read it over, circle the *"but"* words or their equivalents, and identify the thought obstacles to clean up. All you have to do is write down the five most important aspects of your new job and how you feel about achieving each of them. Then look at what statements you made that are obstacles on your path. Where are the branches blown down, and where is the path clear to your destination? Get busy cleaning up your path.

Figure out how you can change your thinking so you no longer have obstacles standing in your way. Yes, this is work:

it takes work to clear the path. But as long as you are in the process of finding a job, you are probably visiting these topics multiple times every day. It is worth clearing the path so it is easy to travel and reach your goal.

Thought Destination #1 of My New Job:

My Thought Obstacles Were:

My New Thinking:

Thought Destination #2 of My New Job:

My Thought Obstacles Were:

My New Thinking:

Thought Destination #3 of My New Job:

My Thought Obstacles Were:

My New Thinking:

Thought Destination #4 of My New Job:

My Thought Obstacles Were:

My New Thinking:

Thought Destination #5 of My New Job:

My Thought Obstacles Were:

My New Thinking:

Create a Picture of Your Success

Visualization is a technique that has been used successfully for many years. You take an image that you want to be real: something you want in your future. Then you project yourself into the image and imagine it *now*, in the present tense, as if you are already living it.

Athletes have used this technique for decades. You visualize where you want the ball to go *before* you put it in motion. You experience yourself delivering the ball right on target. You enjoy the feeling of a successful delivery.

Some people might call this a daydream. You are envisioning it in your mind's eye, inside you. But, unlike most daydreams, this is very intentional. Your mind is not wandering. You are doing this *on purpose*: it is planned. *See it on the inside to achieve it on the outside.*

For instance, let's pretend I have an interview. I usually become very anxious before interviews, especially if I feel I really want/need the job. So I visualize myself walking into the building where the interview is occurring. I am feeling calm, comfortable, confident. I see myself walking into the room and meeting the interviewers. I am still feeling good. I shake hands, make eye contact, remember their names. Then I visualize myself sitting down with these interviewers. I am at ease. The answers to their questions come easily. I am very articulate. My answers are complete, to the point, intelligent and thoughtful. I make a strong case for why I want this job and why I am excited about working for their organization. My enthusiasm is sincere and obvious. I clearly explain the unique contribution I can make, how and why I can effectively produce the results they are seeking. The words and answers flow to me. I leave the interview feeling really positive about my performance.

Once I finish visualizing the interview, I am feeling good. So now I think about how confident I was and how much better I am feeling now, in this moment. I take time to enjoy the good feelings. I think about the interview, and start to link those good feelings with that interview. My associations with that interview begin to shift.

If I have five days until the interview, I practice this visualization two or three times each day. I want this feeling to become natural. This is part of my preparation for the interview.

On the day of the interview, I arrive at the building a few minutes early. I sit in my car and listen to my theme song (or go into a waiting room or rest room in the building if I don't have a car). Then I go through the visualization again. It helps to calm any anxieties. This is now a practiced feeling. I remember this feeling. I have been enjoying practicing for several days. So I reenter the feeling, feel better, and then go into the interview.

When I leave the interview, I remember my general statements of well-being. *It is all going to turn out all right. This is a part of my path to where I want to go. Everything is always working out for me.* I bring myself back to that feeling of well-being. I may listen to my theme song again on the way home.

I may visualize, in advance, my friends asking me about the interview afterward. How did it go? I tell them, "*Great. Everything is working out just fine. It was a wonderful experience. I learned a lot.*" And then I comfortably change the direction of our conversation, because I don't want to dwell on it. My friends mean well, but their worry doesn't feel good to me. I focus instead on their intention, and think what a great experience the interview was. It is nice to have friends who care about me. I release any anxiety, and feel calm again.

Visualizing is a way to prepare for the future before you actually experience it. Think about pilots who sit at flight simulators and learn how to handle difficult situations. The intent is to become so skilled that even in an emergency, they move right into the behaviors they have learned and trained in. The new behaviors have become second nature. Often, affirmations may go along with this. They may be telling themselves: *I know what to do. I have handled this before. I am well-trained for this situation. I know how to respond.*

Consider taking an empty picture frame and putting it somewhere you look regularly. When you see the frame, imagine it holding a photo of you happy at your new job. Imagine the future you want, and see it there. Don't look at the frame as blank: fill it with mental images of what you want. See your future.

You can visualize any situation as you want to live it in your future. Maybe you visualize how you will feel on the day you start your new job. Maybe you visualize what you will say when you get a phone call with a job offer. Take the situation, script it so it feels real, natural and authentic. See yourself living it, but more importantly, *feel* yourself living it. Get inside the visualization and make it real.

What Success Looks Like To Me…

What Success Feels Like To Me…

Affirming What You Want

Affirmations are another useful tool that has been around a long time. But many people misunderstand affirmations, just as they misunderstand visualization. Intentional affirmations are about changing your patterns of thought. They are another way to tell a different story, a new and better story.

An affirmation is a story you tell about a situation. You are making affirmations all day, every day. Every time you tell a story about something in your life, you are affirming it and reinforcing the reality of it.

Let's say I want a job and I don't have a job. How many times a day do I affirm my present situation? I may think about it dozens or more times each day.

So what if I change what I am affirming to: *I am in the process of finding a really great job.* What if I start saying: *I can feel things are turning around for me. I am really looking forward to starting my new job.*

In order to affirm a statement, I need to believe it. If I don't believe the presence of a new job, then I am affirming the lack of it. It is not so much the words as the feeling I give the words.

Do I feel I am actually in the process of finding a new job? Do I have hope that a great job is out there, or have I stopped hoping? Am I really focused on finding a job, or have I become caught up in the process of looking and applying? There is a real difference in finding jobs to apply for, and finding a job to actually work at.

Listen to these two people tell their stories. What do you hear them actually affirming about their present situations?

"Well, I keep looking but I don't know who would want to hire me. I feel out of touch with today's emphasis on social marketing. I don't know how to twit or chirp or whatever it is these young people are doing. Still, I need to find a job. My savings are almost gone."

Now listen to this person: "I have a great job. I don't know where it is yet, but I do know I'm in the process of finding it. It's going to be a wonderful fit for me, and give me all kinds of potential for advancement. I have a lot to offer a company. I'm a very dedicated employee and a hard worker. I learn quickly, and I know I'll move ahead. I'm really excited about the new opportunities awaiting me."

Both people could be viewed as having the same present reality. Neither has a job. But what they are affirming about their present situation is completely different. Which of these two people would you expect to be hired first?

Consider what you are affirming in your life. What do you want to change about your present? What stories do you want to keep affirming in your future? Start listening to yourself when you talk to friends and family, or even when you are thinking about your present situation.

Then ask yourself, what do I *want* to be affirming? What do I want to be living? Start shifting your statements. Keep them present tense. Make them believable: *you* need to *believe* what you are saying. *You* need to *feel* each statement as true.

Some people like to write out these statements and post them in the house or car. Some people put them next to the television, mute the ads and use that as time to repeat the statements. Other people put the statements in their phones, computers, or even use them as screensavers. Keep the statements up only as long as they feel fresh to you. When you realize you have been overlooking a statement for a few days and not paying attention to it, take it down and post a new statement. If posted affirmations become stale or meaningless, it is time to find new ones.

Many people find their affirmations shift over time. You start out affirming the feeling of *enough*, for instance. Then you want a little more, and become comfortable with the idea. You might shift from *I have enough to pay the bills* to *I have more than enough to pay the bills*. As your patterns of thought start to shift and open, you may find your affirmations shifting, too.

My New Affirmations

My affirmations are in the present tense.
The statements are believable to me.
I feel them as though they are already realized.

Expanding Your New Affirmations and Stories

Another approach to deepening the feeling of what you want to achieve is to spend more time in the feeling-place of it.

Think about what you want, and how it will feel when you achieve it. What are the feelings it will produce in you?

For instance, maybe you want a job where you can feel you are making a contribution. *I like knowing I am making a difference. I like the sense of contributing to the success of an organization.*

What are some times in the past that you have had this feeling? For instance, where have you worked or volunteered before and found that sense of being valued? Maybe you were part of a team and liked the sense of doing your part for the success of the team.

Now, get inside that feeling. For instance, if you were part of a high school or college team, what did you enjoy about it? What are the key positive feelings you had? Identify them. Then think of specific examples. *I liked the sense of belonging to a team and contributing to the group effort.* What are some times in your life when you felt you belonged? What are times you enjoyed a sense of contributing to a larger effort? What are memories you have of making a difference for someone?

If you want financial abundance, then what are the feelings you have when thinking about having financial abundance? *I like the ease that comes from knowing I have enough money. There is a freedom in being able to make choices based on what I want, knowing that resources are available. I like the security that comes from knowing money is available.* So the key feelings here are ease, freedom, the ability to make choices, and security. What are examples in your life, or positive associations, you make with each of these feelings?

Remember specific moments as a child when you felt ease. It doesn't have to be a dominant emotion you had as a child. But was there ever a time you felt ease? What was that memory? Get inside that memory and relive it: feel that ease again.

Perhaps you associate freedom with birds that are flying, joyfully riding the breezes just for the fun of it. Think about the freedom to fly above the rest of the world, to go where you want to go. That freedom allows choices. See yourself experiencing that freedom, enjoying that ability. Feel it fully.

Think about what you want to achieve and the feelings that go with it. Identify the key feelings. Then find past memories and experiences, or examples like the bird, that you can easily imagine. Go there in your mind and live these feelings. Start spending time in the feeling-place of what you want every day.

This is more than escape. When we have different emotions, we also think differently. I think differently when I am feeling ease than when I am feeling anxious. If I am feeling fear or panic about something, I may not let solutions come to me. But if I am feeling ease, I am more relaxed, open and creative. Thinking patterns are often tied to our emotional states. By finding desirable emotions and spending time there, we intentionally shift our thinking.

Recreate the feeling of what you want in your mind and your body. Shift your thinking so you start living what you desire. Your attention recently may have been directed at what you lack or feel is missing in your life.

Having a job that you like and the security of reliable income may feel far away from where you are right now. But you can still find the feeling-place of having what you want. You can recreate the feelings of what you want right now.

Start spending time every day in the feeling of what you want. You are retraining your mind and the way you think. You are moving into the feeling and thinking of achieving the success you desire.

Expanding My Affirmations

What are the feelings I want to have in my new job?

What are times in my life when I have had these feelings?
(If you have had each of the feelings in separate experiences,
that's fine too. Just write about the individual experiences.)

What are other positive associations I make with these feelings? (For instance, other images or words, places or memories that come to mind.)

I Am...

Below is a list of more than a hundred words. Most people will find these words to be positive or even very positive. Try to attune yourself to the meaning of the word. Let yourself *feel* it; let yourself *be* it. These words can help replace old recordings you may be trying to find substitutes for. They are words you can focus on if you feel someone is viewing you negatively or if you are viewing yourself negatively. Simply stop the negative thought and redirect your attention to this list. Some of the words will challenge you to attune to the meaning: to be one with it. For instance, it may not make grammatical sense to *be flow...I Am Flow.* But the idea of feeling the movement of the flow of air or water can give the sense of riding a natural current forward, carrying you into what you want in your life.

If a word does not resonate with you, just skip it and go to the next word. Some words may feel differently on different days, depending on your mood. This is a great list to read before you go to bed at night, when you first wake in the morning, or both. They can be helpful words to repeat when you are engaged in activities such as housecleaning, standing in line, or commuting. Find these qualities in yourself. Find these qualities in the people and environment around you. Don't just say the words, but actually feel the meanings.

This exercise is a mental exercise, but it is intended to be fun and uplifting. Play with it. What are your favorite ten or twelve words on the list? What are words you want to live more in your life? This list is not exhaustive. Add words to the list that resonate with you as you think of them. The list is just a starting point.

I AM...

aligned	exhilarated	inspired	phenomenal
allowing	exciting	inspiring	precious
appreciative	engaging	incredible	remarkable
authentic	expansive	intuitive	sure
abundant	evolving	intelligent	satisfied
articulate	expanding	imaginative	spontaneous
beautiful	ecstatic	important	super
blissful	excellent	intentional	superb
bright	encouraging	joyful	special
basking	enthusiastic	kind	thoughtful
beneficent	exuberant	knowing	trusting
blessed	energetic	light	thrilled
blooming	ease	love	thriving
brilliant	fun	loved	talented
cherished	flow	loving	understanding
clear	funny	lively	uplifting
confident	fantastic	magnificent	vital
curious	flourishing	marvelous	vibrant
creative	fulfilled	magnanimous	wise
divine	great	noble	witty
dynamic	grateful	outstanding	well-spoken
delightful	gracious	optimistic	well-being
deliberate	gorgeous	powerful	worthy
delighted	happy	passionate	whole
delicious	hopeful	prosperous	wow
eager	humorous	pleased	yes!
excited	healthy	purposeful	zest

My List of *I AM* Words

Circle your ten or twelve favorite words on the list, or write them here.

What other words do you want to claim? What other positive, uplifting, empowering words describe you?

Success is Your Destination

We often feel a loss of control when we are job hunting: we feel the people hiring are in charge of whether or not we get the job. We don't feel we have any control over the process.

You may not be able to control whether you get a specific job in a specific company. But you do control your future. You do control your own success.

You have to give your attention to what you want and where you want to go. When you get in your car to drive somewhere, you do not keep your attention on where you are. You do not say, "I am in this parking space and this is where I am going to be forever." You think about where you want to go. You may think about different routes to travel, then choose the one you want. You are focused on your destination, not on where your car is parked at the present moment.

If you get in your car and stay focused on where you are, you won't move. You have no need to accelerate. You will simply stay where you are. Your destination is your present moment and your present location. "I am where I am."

If you don't like your current parking space and want to go somewhere else, you need to think about your destination. When you are determined to go somewhere, you find a way. Single-mindedness is about focus: directing your focus to what you want and keeping it there.

Anyone who has intentionally created an invention would tell you that the focus stayed on what was wanted and desired. Inventors often have hundreds if not thousands of failures. People who get discouraged easily don't become inventors. An inventor might say, "I know what I want to do...now how do I get there?" They listen to internal inspiration. They learn through trial and error. But they stay focused on what they want. If they become focused on their failures and the fact they have not become successful yet, they are creating roadblocks to the solutions. They have to stay focused on the destination: on where they are going. Sometimes, through their failures, inventors discover wonderful products and ideas they never thought possible before. But not because they gave up: because they kept going.

When you get an interview, and you will, don't worry about the outcome. Enjoy the process. See the interview as an indicator you are on the path to your destination.

I remember a hiring committee I chaired at a university. We had several applicants come in for interviews. Most of them were dressed properly, knew the "right" things to say, and had the necessary skills. It was also clear that they were anxious about making a good presentation.

Then we had a woman come in who lit up the room. She was different than the other applicants. Rather than feeling like we were getting a version of her that was constricted by fear, we felt like we were seeing her authentic self. She didn't seem afraid of us or of the interview process. She was light and open. Of course, we hired her. Even though she didn't have as much experience as some of the other candidates, this was clearly a woman we wanted in our department.

This woman later told me that she had decided, before coming to the interview, that she knew we were not going to select her. She had been on numerous interviews and not received any callbacks. She had given up the idea this was the only possible job for her. So she thought she would be herself and have fun with the interview process. She had surrendered her need to control, and changed her attitude to: *I am going to enjoy this and have fun with it. I am going to meet new people and learn new things. I am going to find new ways to answer questions about myself, and perhaps gain insight I didn't have before.* We didn't see a version of this woman that was restrained by a fear of pleasing us and saying the "right" thing: we saw *her*. And we loved what we saw.

If we approach interviews in the brilliant way this woman did, we are much more likely to be hired. She did not bring the committee a feeling of desperation. We saw her openness and willingness to learn. She had not given up on her destination, but she had given up on deciding "this is the one path there." She had taken the pressure off herself, and in doing so, had actually shown us more of herself.

Be prepared for your interviews so you feel comfortable. How can you convey your enthusiasm that you truly want this job? How do you make your case that you are a great person for the job? How can you convince them that, a year from now, they will feel good about having hired you? But over-preparation can cause anxiety and fear: you may be trying to remember too much. There is no way to prepare for every question that might be asked. Approach the interview as an opportunity to meet new people and to learn new information, and as an experience to enjoy. Remember that an interview is intended to be a two-way conversation, not an interrogation. What do you want to learn from this interview about your potential employer? You can't anticipate what they are seeking, but you can decide to feel good about how you present yourself. You can find value in the interview process regardless of the outcome.

I remember a position for which I was hired because the interviewer said I knew and understood myself well. "Skills are teachable," she said, "but you have to know your capabilities as well as your limitations. You do." Self-knowledge was more important to her than job knowledge and prior experience.

Interviewers are not always looking for what we think they are. You cannot anticipate the qualities an interviewer is seeking. There are often dimensions to jobs we cannot anticipate. Sometimes they need a person to provide a certain perspective as part of a team. They might want someone with a different background than their current employees. They might be seeking someone process-oriented or data-driven. Perhaps they want someone who fits into the existing culture, or someone who will shake it up. You cannot mind read. And their selection of another candidate over us is not personal, even though it may feel that way. It's important to remember that one interview can help us better prepare for the next. Like the candidate at the university, keep your destination in mind, but surrender what you believe to be the only path there.

There are multiple paths open to us. When we are driving a car and encounter a detour on our journey, we follow it. We don't stop the car and decide not to go further. We are still heading to our destination, just not on the path or time frame we had anticipated. I know I have taken detours on roads that led to wonderful discoveries of places and people I would not have otherwise encountered. I surrendered to the idea I was not on the path I intentionally chose, but I was still progressing to my destination. I surrendered my preconceived idea of the path there, and decided to enjoy where I was. I was still advancing to my destination.

Don't let the interviewer's opinion of you, or your interpretation of what the interviewer thought, decide for you the *value of the interview*, or more importantly, *the value of you*. You know your own self-worth. You know you are a valuable and capable human being.

It can be helpful after an interview to write down a list of the positive qualities of that interview. What did you say that you liked? What did you learn? What did you like about the interview or the environment of the interview? What did you like about the interviewer(s) or the questions? Keep your focus on the positive.

Interviews can also be great learning and preparation tools for future interviews. If you didn't like the way you answered a question, think now, without the pressure, how you would choose to answer it. Create a response you like and write it down. Practice it. You don't want to remember mentally the old answer you gave; you do want to remember the way you would answer it now, and the next time.

Deliberately craft an answer to the question, "How did the interview go?" As mentioned previously, how can you answer truthfully and positively? If you have told friends and relatives you have an upcoming interview, they will probably ask. Be intentional about your answer. "I learned a lot." "It was great to learn more about the organization." "They had some good questions and I was pleased with my answers." "I felt like they got a sense of who I really am." "I showed them I am capable of handling the responsibility with ease." "I really communicated my enthusiasm about the job and the company." Find statements you can feel good about saying that also perpetuate the way you want to feel.

After the Interview

What were some positive qualities of the interview? *How I feel good about this experience...*

What I did that I liked/pleased me...

What I learned...

What I liked about the interviewer...

What I liked about the environment…

What I liked about the questions…

A stronger answer I may use in the future…

"How did the interview go?" *Answering it positively…*

Feeling Successful, Being Successful

When we feel successful, we often want new arenas to be successful in. I may feel successful in my home life and my social life. So how about a new work environment? Maybe I already have a job, but I want a better one. How can I become more successful in my current job until the door to my next opportunity opens?

Have you ever noticed that when people complain about their boss or coworkers and change jobs, within a few months they are repeating the same negative mantras about their new boss and coworkers? We take ourselves wherever we go. If there is something you didn't like about your previous (or current) employment, change the story you are telling and focus on the positive aspects instead.

You can be a successful human being in any environment. You can be successful with or without a job. It doesn't take money to feel successful. It doesn't even take money to be successful. Many of the happiest people alive would tell you they are successful because of the people in their lives, and because of the differences they feel they have made in their communities. They enjoy loving, and they feel loved. They enjoy giving their time and talents, and they feel blessed in return. There are different ways to measure riches.

Decide *now* that you are going to like the next job you have. You are going to find positive aspects there. Whether you feel it is a short-term or long-term position, something to tide you over or a career move you hope to keep until retirement, decide in advance you will like it.

There are many people who focus on the negative aspects of their job, then seem surprised when they're fired or laid off. These people are essentially asking to leave their current job. They are only finding fault with it. They are only finding reasons the job does not serve them.

Have you ever been a passenger in a car where the driver hated detours, and even though taking one was necessary, complained and complained while you took it? You probably never wanted to take a detour with this person again. It is much more fun and enjoyable to ride with someone who finds value wherever he or she is. These are the people we want to be with. These are the people we want to work with. These are the people most organizations want to hire. They want employees to contribute positively to morale, not detract from it.

I remember a woman who was getting ready to move into a nursing home. She described the facility in the most glowing terms. The people were nice and caring. There were lovely decorations to make the rooms attractive. The kitchen did its best to prepare good-tasting meals. Then I found out she had never even visited the facility. How did she know all these positive attributes? She had decided in advance that she would like it, and a positive attitude would make her new "home" work for her. She was going to find the very best in everyone and everything that she could.

Even with a job you don't like, you can decide, "This is where I am, and something better lies ahead. So what can I find to like about where I am?" Liking where you are will help you advance to something new. Until you reach the new place, you might as well find value in the scenery on this detour.

The Path of Least Resistance

When I first earned my bachelor's degree, I couldn't find a job in my field. So I turned to retailing, where I had worked while I was going to school. I thought I would find a job in retail management. Well, the country was in a recession. I couldn't find a management position, or even a full-time position. I finally took a part-time job at a new store that was opening. Some of the full-time staff were new to retailing and didn't like the work. They soon left, so I had a full-time job within weeks. Then an assistant manager quit. I had supervisory experience, so I was given the position. The manager decided she needed to spend more time with her children, so she left the company. Within months, I was working in the management position I had been seeking.

I have long believed in following the path of least resistance. If you imagine a river, you know there can be many turns and bends. I may see only the section of water in front of me when I am standing on the bank looking at it. If we put a boat in the river and climb in, the water is naturally going to carry us to a new destination. But I may not be able to see the whole path of the river. I may know I am embarking on a new journey, but not yet know my final destination.

The path of least resistance is the easiest path to travel between two points: how the water, the natural flow, will carry us. It is when all doors seem closed to us and one opens, but it is not the door we thought we wanted. When I was seeking a retail management position, the only door that opened was a part-time minimum wage job. But it seemed to be the path of least resistance, so I took it. And it turned out to lead to the job I had wanted.

Sometimes we have to step out on faith, especially if it feels right to us. If you have an offer for a job that doesn't make sense logically, but you have a gut feeling you should take it, consider following your instincts. It could be a path to something greater.

If there is a job where you don't meet the minimum qualifications but you feel you should apply, then do. It doesn't hurt to apply. Maybe there is something in your résumé that the hiring manager is seeking but didn't put in the job description. Perhaps the personnel director will have a gut instinct to call you. Maybe there is another position available that isn't even posted yet, and you are perfectly qualified. Maybe the interviewer will ask you a question that you answer incompletely, but it leads you to develop the perfect answer that wins you a job later. When you feel like the river is carrying you toward something positive, try to ride it out. Trust that you don't see all the bends in the river, but that there are bound to be some ahead that will serve you.

Some people will ask, but what if the river is leading to rapids that I can't see? Well, most people on the job market already feel like they are riding the rapids. What if there is smoother water ahead? And do you know how many people pay money every year to be escorted through rapids, because riding the rapids can be fun and exciting?

Trust your instincts, your intuition. Don't let your head determine every turn you make. If I am standing on the bank of the river seeing a small portion of it, I am not seeing the whole river. I can't judge the destination where the river will lead me by the tiny section in front of me. If I look at that small portion of the entire journey and say, "This isn't where I want to be," then I am missing where the river can lead me.

If, however, I think, "I really want to put my boat in this river, and it feels like the right thing to do," then I would trust my judgment. If I go 200 yards and say, "Let me out of this boat because this river isn't moving in the direction I want to go," then I am not allowing the path of least resistance to carry me. Maybe the next bend will bring me to a better place. Maybe there is a much happier, better-paying turn in the river that I simply can't see yet.

I met my husband when I selected a middle seat on an airline flight. It was not a seat I normally would have selected. But when I was picking out a seat for the flight on my computer, that seat lit up for me. It was like the seat was saying, "Pick me!" even though it was not a logical choice.

Don't assume you know where every river is going. Don't assume that the job in front of you is the whole river: it may be one tiny section of it. If I am standing on the banks of the Mississippi River, I might see a mile or less of it. I have no idea how large or mighty the entire river is, or how far the river could carry me. If I thought what I could see was the whole river, I would be greatly mistaken.

There really is no small job. Every job is essential, or it wouldn't exist. I know a man who was once a light bulb changer for a manufacturing company. He said it was a fascinating job. He was allowed to go all over the plant, because there were light bulbs everywhere. He developed friendships with people in many divisions, because he wasn't limited to one. He came to understand what interpersonal dynamics would help him get the job done the first time, instead of being told that room or office was too busy and he would have to come back later. He discovered there was a tremendous variation in light bulbs, and learned which bulb was most effective for which task. People started coming to him to see how he could improve the lighting in their work areas. He said it was a great job, and it was in part because he had a great attitude about it. He had a job he enjoyed, that he felt paid him well and gave him good benefits: a job most of us would not even think existed.

Allow the flow of the river to carry you to what you want. Your intention is clear. If a job opportunity feels right to you, don't try to talk yourself out of it because it is not logical or not what you thought you wanted. The river may hold wonderful surprises ahead.

Hope

Hope.

You have to have hope.

Hope is as essential to the job-finding process as a computer or proper interview attire: maybe even more so.

Hope is also like cork that rises in water: it is natural to us. Hope is innate to who we are as human beings.

But, like the earlier example of cork submerged in water, we can develop beliefs that suppress our hope.

If you have lost hope, you need to find it. You need to go looking for it. Hope is crucial. If a loved one went missing, you would immediately start searching. If you have lost hope, you need to search for it until you find it.

If people advised you that you should give up on finding your missing loved one, you know you would keep searching as long as you felt, inside yourself, that you should. You wouldn't listen to the advice of others. You would listen to your own internal guidance.

Don't listen to family and friends who may be well-intentioned, but have stopped believing in you or your ability to find a job. Don't listen to nay-sayers who tell you to give up. Don't believe someone who says there isn't a job out there for you.

If you're talking with them and that's where the conversation starts to go, intentionally shift it: bring up another subject and divert the direction.

Every time we apply and are not hired, we could give up a little piece of ourselves, a little piece of our hope.

Don't.

This process feels personal, but it isn't.

Hope is your air right now: you need it to survive.

Fortunately, it is also just as readily available as air. And it's free: it doesn't cost a thing.

This age of the internet actually makes hope as easily accessible as everything else in the cloud.

There are videos on web sites like *YouTube* that offer living examples of people who had hope and found what they were searching for. Maybe it was a job. Maybe it was a cure to a disease or condition. Maybe it was a life partner, or a child, or a dog. Maybe it was a new purpose. Web sites like the self-help publisher *Hay House* are filled with books by people who kept hoping and eventually found what they were seeking. Go to web sites like these and look up words like *inspirational, uplifting, encouraging*. (I have no idea what will be posted when you do visit, of course. Sift until you find something positive and of value.) When you do get a job, you may even want to add your own story to help encourage others. Go to the library and ask the librarian what she/he recommends as hopeful or inspirational books, or where in the library you could find some. (Libraries are a great place to go, by the way, if you need a free place to spend some quiet time. Most have computers/printers, *Wi-Fi*, and local periodicals that may have job listings not found online.)

If you aren't ready yet for these kinds of optimistic videos, then look for something *funny*. You need to laugh. We all need to laugh. Watch funny movies or programs on television (and mute any depressing commercials). Find them on the internet. You need to look for reasons to *feel good*. Ask your friends, if you think they would be helpful: what have you seen or heard lately that made you laugh? There is a reason that cute animal and baby videos are so popular: *they help us feel good.* What helps you feel good? Maybe you like funny sports videos. Maybe you like watching old comedies. Maybe you like videos of failed/spoiled magic tricks. Find reasons to laugh, and you are on your way to hope.

Are there ways you can make this job-finding process fun? Yes, I know that question can sound like sacrilege. We're supposed to take job-finding very, very seriously. But remember the story of the woman who went into the interview with plans to enjoy it, because she had surrendered the idea that this was *the job* for her? She gave up on the idea of it being the *only* path, and in reality, the job became part of her journey. She approached the interview genuinely and sincerely, but more lightly. *She* was present, instead of her fear.

How can you start to see the process from a bigger picture, and with a lighter perspective? What aspect would be appealing to you? Some people like to compare job application forms, online personality tests, or waiting rooms in Human Resource departments. What is the lighting like? How does the receptionist greet you? What kind of furniture does the organization have, and how is it positioned? Where is there a clock, if there is a clock? What is hanging on the wall as decoration? Are the offices/cubicles/desks decorated by their inhabitants? These are observations you will probably want to keep to yourself, or at least may not want to share at the prospective job site. But it starts to add another dimension to the process. Instead of focusing on feeling anxious while you wait, you can distract yourself and have some fun with what you choose to observe. (Some ideas: *Hmmm...They positioned that clock so I can't see how long I'm waiting, but the receptionist has a clear view. They did the same thing at the last place I interviewed. Wow! Look at all the photos on the receptionist's desk: what a truly happy-looking family. I bet they have fun times together.*)

Sometimes at interviews, applicants show their fear and anxiety more than their skill and qualifications. You have to believe in yourself. That is part of the reason people with jobs, even jobs they are overqualified for, usually do better at *the next* interview. If you feel you *have* to get that job because you are worried about paying bills or having food on the table, you are putting tremendous pressure on yourself. It may be better to be working somewhere – anywhere -- so you have a little less pressure when you start interviewing for jobs more in line with your desires. It may be better to work a temporary job so you feel employed and know you have some income. *There are no small jobs, only narrow attitudes.* Every job is important and needs to be done or it wouldn't exist, especially in today's marketplace.

Moving Forward

However you have gotten to this point in your journey, I am guessing you do not like the results or you would not be reading this book. Continuing to focus on a problem is very different than generating possible solutions.

If ancient peoples thought about crossing large bodies of water with an expectation of always drowning, they would never have discovered boats. Once people observed that logs floated, it seemed logical that if one were riding on or inside a log, one might float too. But then it was a long time before people realized you didn't have to be riding in wood to float on water: another consideration was the displacement of water. Thus boats could be made of metal and other substances, too.

If ancient peoples kept focusing on the problem, they could never have found a solution.

If you feel like it is difficult or impossible to get a job, you need to look up from the rut you are standing in. See the horizon? See everything that lies before you? Now, how are you going to get there?

The most important thing to realize in this moment is that *a solution exists.* But you can't keep looking down at the rut and move out of the rut at the same time. Nor can your friends and family help you move if you have become so accustomed to where you are planted that you are not willing to try a different approach.

In truth, more than one solution exists. There are the roads well-traveled and the roads less-traveled. There is the horizon to your front, but there is horizon all around you.

Whatever approach you have been taking, it may be time to consider something different. It may mean re-creating your résumé and taking a fresh perspective in your cover letter, learning to answer questions in a new way, wearing different interview attire. It may mean finding new sources of job listings, getting busy networking, or expanding your pool of references. It may mean that you consider jobs or fields you haven't applied for before, or that you think about going back to school. Maybe you contemplate volunteer work or internships. Or perhaps you consider how you could create your own business and develop your own source(s) of revenue apart from traditional jobs.

I have always liked Joseph Campbell's advice to "follow your bliss." Do any of the ideas above, or others that may come to you, help you feel inspired to take action? Do any of these roads feel better to you? Maybe you think, "I could do that," or "That one sounds appealing." Perhaps you reach out for help, asking a friend who has done hiring to look at your résumé. Maybe you contact a counselor, or ask for help at your place of worship: *I am ready to do something different. I am ready to try a new path.*

Have you ever picked up a child who didn't want to be picked up and was fighting you? That is a very different experience from picking up that same child who is happy and asking to be picked up. The child who is in a reluctant mood always feels a lot heavier than the happy child!

Are you ready to move forward? Do you want to?

Decide today, now, that you are ready for a shift. You have been working at exercises to help you think and feel differently. Now, you are ready to create new results. No more ruts. No more looking at where you are. Starting in this moment, decide you are going to move forward into your future and claim it. You are going to move ahead into all the good things that await you. You are ready for your present and recent past to become a memory, and one you don't think about anymore! You are focusing on your future, and opening yourself to new paths to travel there.

The world is full of new paths and paths not yet taken. Often, we don't see them because we are looking at the old paths, the old ruts. You have tremendous ability to create what you want in your life. You have unique contributions to make *that no one can make but you.*

Your future is your legacy. Your creation and living of the future you want will speak volumes to the people who know you and the people you have yet to meet. You did not give up when times became rough. You simply found new paths to take. You cleared new paths where old ones didn't exist. You found new paths of thought that helped reaffirm what you are capable of. You knew that this period of unemployment did not represent who you are and what you have to offer. Now you are moving out, moving ahead. You are showing the world the new you.

When you think differently, you see solutions instead of problems. When you think differently, you figure out new paths you can take instead of relying on the paths people took before you. When you think from a perspective of success and do not accept failure as an option, you will find new doors opening. And if those doors don't open at first, you will find different doors that do.

This is not an experiment. This is your life. This is the life you are living and the life you are creating. You know you have a lot to offer. You know you are worthy of wonderful things happening in your life. To begin, all you have to do is look up from the rut and decide how you are going to move forward into the rest of your life. *Then do it.*

Keep reviewing your lists of successes and abundant moments. Keep in touch with the part of you that knows *I can do it, and I am doing it.* Keep working the exercises as long as it takes for you to connect with your legacy of success.

You are the only person who determines what you think. You are the only person who controls your thoughts. Don't let anyone else determine your worth: *they can't.*

We live what we believe to be true.

Stay focused on your destiny, but allow for inspiration about how to get there. Allow that there are many paths, not just one. Trust in your ability to do it.

If you have anxieties about taking a new job, be honest with yourself and make peace with them. If you are concerned about being successful in your new position, decide you will do the best you can. If you are worried about the hours a new job may require you to be away from your family, consider how you will be providing even better for them and decide to plan a vacation, even a "stay-cation" at home, that will allow you special time to bond. It will be something you can look forward to. If there are thoughts standing in your way of completely dedicating yourself to finding a new job, examine them, make peace with them, and let them go. Also consider that there may be a way around those issues that you have not seen yet, from your place of focusing on the problem.

People will often say to me, "I want to feel better, and I will as soon as I find a new job." The challenge is in feeling better *before* finding the next job. When you stay focused on the lack of a job, you are staying focused on the problem. When you start to feel better *now,* you allow yourself to begin finding solutions.

Often, we end up in our current situations through a gradual process similar to erosion. Would you intentionally choose to live the life you are living today? Or would you choose to live differently? If someone gave you a book of model lives, the way people seeking a new home see model apartments or houses, would you select the model you are currently living? If the answer is a strong *NO,* then think about what model you would select. How can you get out of this rut and begin moving toward living the life you want?

No matter how you are living today, you can choose to think differently. No matter what your present circumstances, you can choose to feel differently. You may have been creating your life by default, as most of us do. So start being intentional in what you think. Begin choosing your thoughts, instead of simply observing what comes along. Be mindful. Start telling positive stories about your present and future.

If you have ever been in a sports stadium, you know there are many places where you can turn your attention. Most people look at the players closest to the ball. But there are other places to look, too. There are the teams and their benches. There are the coaches and other players. There are the fans. There may be cheerleaders and musicians. There may be groundskeepers, vendors or news media. There may be friends/family/colleagues who attend the game with you. There is also the rest of the environment: one can look up or around instead of down or ahead. There are many places to direct your attention, and you are choosing where you focus.

Any place you are has multiple potential places to focus. You choose what you look at. You choose where you direct your attention. Consider the internet. The internet is approaching a half billion web sites. Most people have a dozen or less they look at routinely. You have not seen most of what is out there. *Why?* (This is a question to consider, and *not* an internet challenge!)

If you are giving your attention to what interests you and resonates with you, then consider if those points of focus are giving you the life you want. If they aren't, you may want to try expanding or shifting what you are thinking.

How are you feeling about yourself these days? Does what you are giving your attention to feel like an accurate representation of who you are: not your present circumstances, but that worthy, deserving essence of you? That inner essence knows what you are truly capable of: to what would that part of you choose to give attention?

You have to be your best friend. You have to be your best motivator. You have to be your best inspirer. You have to be the one who says: I am making a change for a better life *today*! You are the only one who chooses what you think. You are the only one who can create a better future for yourself and the people important to you.

Sometimes, people say they fear success. When you fear success, you not only deprive yourself: you also deprive the people who would benefit from your success. There are people you will serve in your career, people who will learn from your example, and people you care about like family and friends. There may be organizations that would benefit from contributions you would make. Some people say they fear making "too much" money, because they equate money with success or have other unresolved associations. A fear of making money can impede your career. Besides, if you have unresolved issues about money, you are preventing yourself from potentially helping people and organizations who may need you.

You alone may determine whether or not you move ahead, despite and through any fear and doubts. But you are not the only one to benefit *because* you move ahead.

Be selfish about being of value to others. Be selfish about your success because you have value to share. You have a unique contribution to make because of who you are and the life you have lived that no one can make *but you*.

The Next Step

Success consciousness is developing an awareness that focuses on success: thinking as though you are already successful. You want to create the energy of success: a state of being where you feel successful. From that state of being, the thoughts, inspirations and actions you have will align with success.

You must believe that you are successful. If you aren't pleased with recent accomplishments in your life, then don't look at them. Look to that inner knowing you do have that you are meant to be successful in your life. Life is supposed to go well for you. There is a part of you that knows unemployment (or underemployment) is only a temporary condition, no matter how long it has lasted. Better things await you. Know it. Find the feeling of it. Believe it. In your heart, you are a successful human being.

Once you believe it, then think from that state of success. How does a successful person think? Well, you are a successful person. You have success in your past and in your future. How do you think when there is something you desire, and you are determined to succeed? How do you approach the discovery of a solution?

When you have a desire for success and a belief in your own success, you will start to expect it. You will start to expect better results: perhaps results that are different than you have been experiencing recently. Once you have an expectation of success, you will set out to achieve it.

Short-term failures are simply opportunities to learn. Then you can spring forward and take a leap based on that growth. Short-term failures simply provide new opportunities to succeed in even better ways. If you learn from a failure, then it is not, by definition, a failure: it is a step forward on your path of success.

You are only limited by your own limitations of thought. Since you placed the limitations there, you can lift them. Since you are the one who keeps telling the old stories in your mind, you can create new stories. You can expect greater things of yourself. You can expect greatness of yourself.

There are exciting, joyful, prosperous times ahead. Keep your focus on what you are becoming and where you are going, not on where you presently are.

I have spoken to people who said they felt like they were beaten down, pushed back into the earth itself. And I reminded them: that is what we do with seeds when we want them to grow. We don't just scatter the seeds in the wind. We push them down into the earth. We want the roots to have something to grab and hold onto while they grow.

When we plant those seeds, we step out on faith for a while. We expect the seeds to grow, but we don't see progress right away. Changing your thinking is a lot like that. You need to start practicing new patterns of thought so you feel successful. But don't dig the seeds up the next morning to see if they have started to grow yet. You have to trust the process. If you feel better and you know better things await you, then trust: better times do lie ahead. If you truly recognize that you are successful, and you expect the seeds to grow, then keep believing. It may be days or weeks before we see sprouts start to come through the earth. But they do.

You know what those seeds are capable of becoming. You know the vision you have of your life.

We don't see the seeds where they are. We don't look at the seeds in our hands and think, "You don't look like much!" We know the potential of the seeds. We know what they can become. And we believe in them.

If you believe in the power of a handful of seeds, don't you think you should believe in yourself? Don't you believe you have much greater potential to rise to?

Let your own greatness out! Feel it. Believe it. Know it to be true.

When you plant those seeds, you make sure they have enough water. They need sun. They need nourishment to grow and survive. What kind of nourishment do you need? How can you nourish yourself and your belief in your own success?

Keep practicing the exercises in this book that you feel are beneficial. Spend time every day nourishing your own greatness, nourishing your own success.

You have every right to be the incredible person that you are. In fact, don't accept less from yourself. Don't allow yourself to be less than you are capable of.

When you plant the seeds, do you want them to grow just a little, or do you want them to develop into all they are capable of becoming? You know it takes time. But you will nurture those plants while they grow. You may want them to grow faster, but you know you need to be patient. Nurture yourself, too. Be patient with yourself. It does take time. But if you know you are on the right path, then believe in your own growth. Believe you are on the journey to becoming everything you know that you are capable of. Don't let yourself settle for anything less. Seeds don't ask if they are worthy of growing. They don't struggle and question,

"Am I deserving of the future I want?" If the seeds don't, why should you?

Those plants have an internal knowing of how to grow and become the best they can be. So do you. You are a success. You are worthy. You are moving into the fullness of all you can become. Be the amazing version of yourself you are intended to be. Claim the successful future you want, and live it.

This is not an end.

Congratulations on your progress, and on creating

a new beginning.

This is your new beginning,

your journey into success.

The best is coming…

Appendix I: When Someone You Love is Unemployed

Sometimes it is very challenging when someone you love and care about is unemployed. What can you do? How can you be supportive? If someone is experiencing low self-esteem or other negative emotions from the loss of a job or underemployment, or is spending an extended time searching for a new job, you may be helpful.

Depending on your relationship to the person who is unemployed, the unemployment, or lack of income, may also affect your life. Over time, it can be easy to let frustration, resentment, fear, anger, or other strong emotions develop.

So, how can you be supportive?

First, you need to have a clear intention that you want to be supportive. This means that you do not blame, criticize or condemn the person. You do not weave negative emotion into statements that appear to be supportive at their surface. You decide, very clearly, that you want to offer emotional support. Period.

Second, you have to release what you think the person should be doing to find a job. This is your loved one's job-finding process. It is not yours. Is it affecting you? Probably a great deal. But you can not take over the job search like it is your own.

If your loved one lost a job, or it is taking longer than expected to find one, your loved one is likely feeling that he or she has lost a certain amount of control. Having someone else step in and try to take over can exacerbate that feeling of being out of control. It may be tempting to you, but don't do it.

If your loved one asks for your help in the job finding process, then discuss exactly what he or she means. What kind of assistance is being requested? Don't step outside the parameters of the role he or she defines for you.

Third, do not offer unsolicited advice. Yes, you probably intend to be helpful. But only offer advice if, and when, it is asked for. Otherwise, keep your advice to yourself.

If you are someone who believes it is helpful to offer unsolicited advice, and you do it frequently, you may want to wear a comfortable elastic band or bracelet on your wrist as a reminder. Every time you feel advice rising in your throat, look at the band instead, or touch it. You need to redirect those words into silence and transform the thoughts into support.

When people want advice and are in a place to really receive and hear what you have to say, they will usually ask for your opinion or your guidance. If they are not asking, they may not be ready or wanting it, no matter how much they love you.

I have known spouses who forcefully intervened in a husband or wife's job search and had unproductive results. Even if the partner found a job as the result of the intervention, it was often not a job that was wanted or that created happiness and success. It can be easier for someone to receive help from a stranger than a spouse.

Fourth, you need to re-envision this person you love. You need to remember his or her strengths. You need to remember positive attributes. You may want to do the exercises in the early part of this book about your loved one. Remember times he or she was successful, resilient. If there were times as a couple or family you experienced greater financial affluence, remember those and the journey there. You need to realize, yourself, that this situation is temporary.

After you do these exercises and make these lists, you may want to share them with your loved one. If your loved one knows you are seeing him or her positively, it can help boost self-esteem and self-image.

If this loved one is a son or daughter, you have to remember that this person is in an adult role now. As much as any parent wants to intervene and be helpful, it is important that you show your belief in your son or daughter's ability to be successful. Find reasons to affirm why you are proud of him or her.

If this loved one is a partner, you may want to spend time recalling when you first met and fell in love. Recall why you came to love this person, and why you were attracted. Remember all the qualities this individual had, and has, that you really appreciated and valued. You might want to plan a date night when the two of you can spend time together. Dates don't have to be expensive: just quality time spent together. Even a walk in a park or a picnic can be fun.

Fifth, you should not put your own life on hold. If you put your own life on hold because of your loved one's unemployment, you may develop resentment about it. Because one of you is going through a challenging time does not mean it should be equally difficult for both of you. Do not feel like your own life should not continue moving forward. It needs to. You need to. Your loved one already feels badly enough. If he or she sees your life suffering because of this period of unemployment, those feelings will only get worse.

If you and your partner have children, do not put their lives on hold – as much as possible. Have an age appropriate discussion with them, based on what they need to know. Explain this is a temporary challenge. Millions of people in this country are experiencing similar challenges. No one did anything wrong. This is simply how it is right now.

Explore alternatives for the children's expenses. There are often scholarships or reduced fees available for summer camps and after school activities. Perhaps your child qualifies for reduced book fees or even free meals at school. If you have children in college, or getting ready for college, contact a counselor at high school or a financial aid counselor at the college your child attends, or hopes to attend. If your first contact with a counselor is not fruitful, try again until you find someone helpful. There may be additional scholarships or loans available if your financial situation has changed. If you see the situation as temporary and without shame, so will your children. Be matter-of-fact about it, while still being sensitive to their concerns.

No one has failed. No one is being punished. Your family is in an unfortunate situation, but you will get out of it and recover. You are modeling for your children how a family can pull together during tough times. You are teaching them for the future, as well as the present.

If you need to meet with a financial or credit counselor about your family's situation, do it. Meeting with a financial or credit counselor does not require a commitment, and should not require a fee. It helps to know what options are available, even if you don't need to take advantage of them right now. If you are someone who finds knowledge empowering, then learn about those options. It is better if you can do this together. If you must go alone, you will have to decide what and when to share with your loved one.

If your loved one is experiencing financial difficulty and you are considering making a loan, there are several things to consider. Do not put your personal financial situation in jeopardy. Do not sacrifice money you have saved for retirement. Do not sacrifice money you have reserved for your children's education. While you may hope and expect that you will be paid back, you need to consider what it will mean if you are not. If you have agreed to co-sign a loan, you should make the payments yourself and have your loved one give the money for the payments to you. Do not put your credit rating in jeopardy. Do not co-sign for a loan payment you cannot afford to make on your own. Loved ones may have the best and most sincere of intentions. But life doesn't always work out as planned. There is nothing wrong with helping someone if you can. It is a generous and honorable thing to do. But only extend yourself as far as you are comfortable. Only loan what could be a gift. Resenting your loved one is not helpful to anyone.

Sixth, maintain your hope. Don't focus on regrets. Don't worry about what might come in the future, if it hasn't yet. Worrying is not productive. Find solutions to your questions and anxieties, but don't dwell on them. Don't give in to the temptation to "what if... these things go wrong" or if the period of unemployment is much longer than you are anticipating. Sometimes we "catastrophize" the future if we do not see a plan or a way out, or through. Focus your thoughts and your attention in helpful ways, not worrisome ways. Expect life to get better.

Seventh, reminisce about the good times. If the present is not pleasing to look at, direct your thoughts to better times, whether they are past or future. Remember times in your life you were happy and experiencing less stress. You may want to put photographs on display of positive times you

171

remember: times that make you smile when you think of them. You may not be able to afford a vacation like you have taken in times past. But you have memories, and possibly photographs or videos. Make a video of places you have visited, or would like to, or find videos online. Put together a video of happy times past, special occasions, or vacations past. Escape there in your mind. It can feel like a vacation, and it doesn't cost anything.

Bring up those happy moments in conversations. When you have a meal together, you can say something like, "I was remembering the other day about the time we..." or "I came across a photograph yesterday about the trip we took." If you have videos or home movies of happy times you experienced, watch them together.

It doesn't cost money to plan a future trip or vacation. You may not know when you will take the trip, and there is no need to think about dates. But just the act of planning can be a lot of fun, and a great diversion from challenging times.

If you feel sometimes like your loved one is a stranger, find happy, or at least neutral, ways to reconnect. Do something together that is unrelated to a job search or to unemployment or financial struggles: something enjoyable and fun. Take a vacation from your troubles, and find ways to enjoy life and each other again.

If you or your loved one is suffering from depression, get help. Sometimes, when people receive treatment for depression and start feeling better, life turns around. We often think, "It will be better when I get a job." But often we need to feel better first so that we can find a job. When we stay focused on problems, it can be hard to see solutions. Depression is not a sign of weakness. It is simply an indication that times have been hard, and life feels off its desired track. It is normal, and nothing to feel shame about.

It is natural that someone who has experienced a trauma like the loss of a job may require some time to get back on his or her feet. But if weeks turn into months, and your loved one is not genuinely trying to improve the situation, there is a problem. Counseling may be needed. If your loved one won't seek counseling, you may want to consider it for yourself. If nothing else, a therapist may provide a neutral perspective on the situation. You can vent frustrations and concerns it may not be helpful to share with your loved one. You may find new perspectives. You can get support that you need. Sometimes, we need support first before we can provide it to someone else.

Eighth, you can be a role model for your loved one. If your loved one sees you dealing positively with challenging times, it may inspire him or her to do the same. If you think positively and expect life to turn around and get better, the feeling may become contagious. If you get help to deal with a problem, it may show your loved one that assistance is available and there is nothing wrong with seeking it. If you don't find shame in the situation, it sends a message to your loved one that you are not blaming.

The underlying current of all these points assumes that your loved one wants life to get better, wants to get a job or otherwise create a reliable source of income. If that is not the case, then you need to return to the fifth point: don't put your life on hold. Get help when you need it. Your loved one, a competent adult, is responsible for his or her own self, and for his or her own life. Do what feels comfortable to be supportive. But you do not want to see your loved one as an anchor that is dragging your own life down if he or she is not trying to improve the situation. You will resent it. Problems will arise in the relationship.

If there were significant challenges with your loved one's previous job, he or she may be wary of entering a difficult job situation again. Listen for how your loved one is envisioning a future job. Is it something to look forward to, or is there a feeling of dread? Is your loved one excited about finding a new job and looking forward to all that may be accomplished, or feeling like a new job means a loss of freedom and control? If there are fears keeping your loved one from moving forward, it can be helpful to identify them and address them.

The most important thing you can do for your loved one is to continue loving and seeing the best in him or her. Let positive qualities dominate your vision.

To summarize the points made above, here are some ways to be helpful to a loved one who is in the process of finding a new job:

1) Be clear you want and intend to be supportive. Avoid blame and criticism.
2) Let go of the temptation to take over your loved one's job search.
3) Don't offer unsolicited advice.
4) Re-envision this person you love, focusing on the positive qualities he or she has.
5) Don't put your life on hold.
6) Maintain your hope.
7) Reminisce about the good times. If the present is not pleasing to look at, direct your thoughts to better times, whether they are past or future.

8) Be a role model. Let your own attitude, behavior and beliefs inspire.

The bottom line is: think positively. Think positively of yourself. Think positively of your loved one. Think positively about the future. No, it is not always easy to do. But it is vitally important to see a happier future. Hope is not a luxury but a necessity.

You need your vision to shine brightly on the days when life seems darkest. You can be the beacon that calls a bright future into your life. You can inspire the best from your loved one if you keep seeing the best there. You have to take care of yourself in order to be there for someone else. You have to believe the future is bright before you can convince anyone else of that. Let the brilliance of your vision be what dominates your time together. Your future shines before you like a guiding light. See it. Follow it. Believe.

Appendix II: Personal Note from the Author

Thanks for buying and reading this book! I hope you find it helpful as you move forward in your journey of finding a great new job. I decided to write this book after I saw these principles working for people who were taking my classes in self-empowerment. I am very interested in understanding how people create the lives they live. It is my intention to help people understand the creative process and how they can be more purposeful in what they are creating. We often create our lives through default, without much deliberate thought about the long-term effects of where we are directing our attention. Paying attention to our present situation affirms it, which serves to perpetuate it. Without changing the way we think, and where we direct our attention, we often keep re-creating the past and reliving it in the present, even if it is not what we want.

If you change your thinking, you really can change your life. Thinking differently allows the entrance of new thoughts and ideas. You can find inspiration where you have not before. You can find new opportunities presenting themselves. You can find yourself newly energized to take action in ways that benefit you and others.

I hope you find the tools in this book to be valuable. A tool is only useful when used. I am hoping that some or all of the tools in this book can be beneficial to you.

I wish you great success as you move ahead. I really do believe that every individual is destined to be successful in his or her life. When we are not, it is simply that our thinking has gotten out of alignment. A car out of alignment has trouble moving quickly down the road: so do we. Everyone has greatness inside. Everyone is capable of much more than we usually let ourselves believe. Believe in yourself, and let your greatness illuminate your life.

Notes

www.ingramcontent.com/pod-product-compliance
Lightning Source LLC
Chambersburg PA
CBHW031958190326
41520CB00007B/286